"Friendless American Male! Not me!"

What kind of friends *do* you have? Work friends, sports friends, camping friends. . . . Who would you turn to if your whole world caved in? Who would you trust enough to share your most intimate thoughts, feelings, frustrations, fears and failures?

In a practical, easy-to-understand way this book presents how men can move toward genuine, intimate friendships. You don't have to "tough" it alone. It's OK to develop relationships with others beyond surface contact.

THE FRIENDLESS AMERICAN MALE

DAVID W. SMITH

FOREWORD BY JIM CONWAY

A Division of GL Publications
Ventura, CA U.S.A.

The foreign language publishing of all Regal books is under the direction of GLINT. GLINT provides financial and technical help for the adaptation, translation and publishing of books for millions of people worldwide. For information regarding translation, contact: GLINT, P.O. Box 6688, Ventura, California 93006.

Scripture quotations in this publication, for the most part, are from the *New International Version*, Holy Bible. Copyright © 1978 by New York International Bible Society. Used by permission. Other versions include:
RSV—Revised Standard Version of the Bible, copyrighted 1946 and 1952 by the Division of Christian Education of NCCC, U.S.A., and used by permission.
TLB—The Living Bible, Copyright © 1971 by Tyndale House Publishers, Wheaton, Illinois, Used by permission.
TEV—Good News Bible, the Bible in Today's English Version. Old Testament copyright © American Bible Society 1966, 1971, 1976. Used by permission.
Phillips—The New Testament in Modern English, Revised edition, J.B. Phillips, Translator. © J.B. Phillips 1958, 1960, 1972. Used by permission of Macmillan Publishing Co., Inc.
KJV—Authorized King James Version.

Published by Regal Books
A Division of GL Publications
Ventura, California 93006
Printed in U.S.A.

Library of Congress Cataling in Publication Data
Smith, David W., 1943-
    Friendless American male.

    Includes bibliographical references.
    1. Men—United States.   2. Friendship.   I. Title.
HQ10901.3.S63   1983   305.3'1'0973   82-21518
ISBN 0-8307-0863-4

Contents

I dedicate this book to
Lee Landeck
who is 85 years old and has been my friend
for 27 years

Foreword

The American male is lonely and friendless, but must maintain his macho image at all costs, even if it means isolation from people. The author of this book is concerned for this man. With a warm, personal, and vulnerable attitude, David Smith presents the situation in the reasoned, documented manner of a social scientist, yet with illustrations and insights that give light and guidance. Dr. Smith is writing from his own personal experience and from information gleaned from 400 interviews.

Some books for men are ego-centristic, teaching men how to look out for themselves and how to win in the cannibalistic world of business. David Smith, instead, points to the biblical models of men in deep, caring relationships with each other and with other people.

Smith's book is not macho, effeminate, or anti-woman. He sees men needing to grow in caring and having deep friendships in order to become whole persons. Women, as well as men, will get a more complete understanding of male needs, fears, and insecurities, as well as their abilities for relationships. An especially strong and practical section is "The Stages of Friendship" where the reader is coached about the development of close, personal friendships.

As you read, you will be convinced that it's OK to be male and to experience warm, caring friendships. IT's not just OK, it's necessary!

Jim Conway
President, Mid-Life Ministries
Assoc. Professor, Talbot Theological Seminary
Author, *Men in Mid-Life Crisis*

Preface

When an author tells his readers that something is wrong with the way they get along with others, but that change can occur if they are willing, these readers have the right to know something about the author and his thoughts up front, before they expend any reading time.

Why this book?

Much is known about the many relationships we experience as adults. Writers and scientists alike have provided the public with abundant information dealing with marriage, family, sexuality, old age, stress, joblessness, in-laws, workaholism and countless other topics.

Doesn't it seem strange that little knowledge and few publications exist which provide us with an understanding of the dynamics of male friendships? Most everyone has opinions and prejudices on this subject, but actual research has been conducted by very few people.

How many friends do people have? Do women have more friendships than men? Why are friendships with the opposite sex so rare? How does age or marital status affect friendships? These are interesting and important questions but this significant aspect of adult life is uncharted with reliable information.

I wanted to conduct my own research, including interviews, in an effort to shed some light on what men and women think and how they behave within the context of friendship. What I discovered is reported in this book.

I am aware that any aspect of human behavior, including attitudes relating to friendship, are quite complex and therefore difficult to correctly analyze. Therefore, the information I acquired during interviews, along with my commentary, will have some limitations. I do feel however that the findings generally reflect the feelings of men and women in America.

I interviewed personal friends, neighbors, members of my church and some of my colleagues at work. But almost all of my questionnaires were given to complete strangers. Strangers are often more honest I found. They have no image or reputation to protect since they don't know you and know they'll probably never see you again.

I talked with 400 people, both men and women, young and old, rich and poor, married and divorced, well educated and not so well educated, Christian and non-Christian. Primarily I talked with people at shopping centers. Individuals passing by were asked if they would mind taking a few minutes to share their views on a questionnaire dealing with friendship. What follows includes the responses of all these people.

I have written this book not so much as a social scientist but as a man who has experienced hurts and frustrations of unrealized or unfulfilled friendships. I have also known the joy and satisfaction that come from being spiritually and emotionally close to a friend. I suppose that more of what and who I am as a man is revealed in these pages than I originally intended. I, like most American men, am reticent about revealing much of my true self, but writing a book about male friendship requires that I be honest and open.

I want to share with you from my experiences and the experiences of others. I have tried to avoid offering a simple, hackneyed or dogmatic formula for improving relationships. This book represents only one stage of my search for better relationships with others. I'm an impatient person, too preoccupied. I still allow a busy life to get in the way of giving and receiving friendships. But I'm getting better at learning how to be a friend to others.

What do I believe?

1. God wants us to have close friendships with other men.

2. Friendships where we give and receive are essential to spiritual and emotional health.

3. Most men in most cases are actually friendless, and have much to learn in the development of interpersonal relationships.

4. Men, including Christian men, lead lives that conform largely to our macho-dominated culture rather than to the Bible.

5. Women tend to experience more fulfilling friendships than do men, and the reasons are not inherent to their biology.

6. Biblical principles of friendship can be identified and, if implemented, can change lives. The Bible offers the best psychology on friendships.

7. Those who possess close nurturing friendships have many personality traits in common.

8. With the decline in the social stability of the extended kinship, family, and the nuclear family itself, friendships are becoming more important socially for mental and spiritual health, and as an area of service and ministry.

I want to express my gratitude to many friends who have shared with me from their hearts about friendship and friendlessness. I thank them for their openness and candor. I want also to express my appreciation to the hundreds of strangers who took the time to be interviewed or to complete a questionnaire for this book. I have learned much from these people.

Finally, I want to acknowledge my indebtedness to my wife and closest of friends, Sue Ann Smith. Without her support, patience, and typing, this book may well not have reached a successful conclusion. Surely without her willingness to listen, discuss, and comment on an endless list of issues related to the book during the last three years, I know the book's final form would have been of lesser quality.

Chapter 1
The Best Property of All

"We take care of our health, we lay up money, we make our roof tight, and our clothing sufficient, but who provides wisely that he shall not be wanting in the best property of all—friends?" *Ralph Waldo Emerson*

"What's all the fuss about? I'm doing just fine. I have all the friends I need." This was one man's response when I asked him about the subject of friendships among men. His wife confided with me later that while he had numerous drinking buddies, he didn't really have even one true friend.

Men are different from women, for which we all give thanks. Unfortunately some of the differences between the sexes are far from being positive. Men have different problems than women, many of which are self-inflicted and therefore avoidable. One serious problem is the friendless condition of the average American male. Men not only perceive friendships differently, their entire way of thinking is often unlike their female counterparts. In asking adult men if they had any close friends, author Herb Goldberg found that many seemed surprised by the question. "No, why? Should I?" was the usual response. Goldberg wonders if men perceive their isolation, their lack of friendship with other men as normal.

Some distinctly male characteristics are of course natural and good (see chapter 3), while others tend to be harmful. These first chapters explore why many men live in such a way that they hinder or even prevent the making and keeping of close friendships with other men.

What are some of the barriers to true friendship?

Aversion to Showing Emotions

Very early in life little boys receive the cultural message that they are not supposed to show emotions. Expressing feelings is generally a taboo for males. Boys soon learn to dread the words, "Don't be a sissy"; "Big boys don't cry"; "Aren't you a little too old to be sitting on your father's lap?" Other messages come through loud and clear—boys must learn to be men. And to be a man means you conceal your emotions.

In the mid 1970s America witnessed on network television the return of many Vietnam-ravaged prisoners of war. Some of these POWs had not been seen by family or friends for a decade. Many relatives had feared the worst—that the one they loved and missed so much might even be dead. Therefore, the long-hoped-for reunions were packed with emotions. Yet mothers and fathers often reacted differently as they saw their sons for the first time in years. Mothers and wives were much more open with their expressions of emotion, but—while there were exceptions—fathers were more reserved. I watched one father on TV simply extend his hand to the son he had not seen in years.

With the exception of acts of violence or in sports,

such as wrestling, men do little touching of one another. Touching implies to many men sexual interest. The thought that someone could want to hug or caress you as an expression of affection or friendship without sexual overtones is hard to believe. Some men become irritated or, more likely, embarrassed if they are hugged by a friend. Perhaps men shun physical expressions of feelings with men because of the unconscious fear of latent homosexual tendencies. Boys learn early in life that males are not supposed to touch each other. Fathers hug their daughters, but at best only rough and tumble with sons. Mock fighting is common with fathers and sons.

This aversion to showing their feelings of affection is a very common barrier to finding or becoming a friend.

Inability to Fellowship

Men find it hard to accept that they need the fellowship of other men. The simple request, "Let's have lunch together" is likely to be followed with the response, "Sure, what's up?" The message is clear: the independent man doesn't need the company of another man. In fact, the image of the independent man is that he has few if any emotional needs. Therefore, men must manufacture nonemotional reasons for being together—a business deal must be discussed or a game must be played. Men often use drinking as an excuse to gather together. Rarely do men plan a meeting together simply because they have a need to enjoy each other's company.

Even when men are frequently together their social interaction begins and remains at a superficial level. Just how long can conversations about politics and sports be nourishing to the human spirit? The same male employees can have lunch together for years and years and still limit their conversation to sports, politics, and dirty jokes and comments about the sexual attractiveness of selected female workers in their office or plant. They do not know how to fellowship.

Inadequate Role Models

Our TV and movie heroes help to perpetuate the male problem of friendlessness. Heroes tend to be self-sufficient, strong and impersonal. They usually lack long-range emotional entanglements. Personalities such as James Cagney, John Wayne, or James Bond are examples of hard, independent men who use rather than love both women and men. They neglect or ignore children. Even in the 1980s men who spend too much time with kids are believed to be effeminate.

The few emotions these role models provide are anger and bravery. In the classic film *High Noon*, Gary Cooper epitomized masculinity in a supreme display of bravery. When he was challenged, his girl implored him to avoid the fight, but he felt he had no choice. While all others turned away in cowardice, Cooper, against insurmountable odds, stood alone against a gang of thugs. This image of manliness is quite rigid and difficult to live up to in real life.

Our movie heroes are usually violent. While many television programmers are recently turning more to displays of cheap sex to attract viewers, there remain many of the so-called action shows which reveal our respect or at least our enjoyment of violent acts. Television programming leads and reflects public opinion. Certain shows like *The Incredible Hulk* illustrate the fascination and respect for violence. How does one solve problems? The hero gets angry and becomes violent. One learns that problems can be solved quickly (the average show is 60 minutes in length) if one becomes physical. Patience, compromise, and long-suffering are seldom traits of those who are masculine.

In real life a cult of toughness has led many men to respond to a real or fantasized challenge to their manliness in ways that are actually dangerous. Many men are ready to respond to a dare, or what seems to be a challenge to their pride. Who participates in barroom brawls? Who tries to cut off another motorist? Who engages in insult trading or shouting matches? Of course, women are capable of physical violence, but usually it is the man who is most willing to turn to violence to settle an issue. Men tend to believe that within the "real man" the capacity for violence is natural.

Sadly, the mask of aggressiveness and strength tends to keep us from knowing ourselves or each other. Fears, joys, loves, hopes, and concerns are largely kept within, preventing men from forming close friendships.

Inordinately Competitive

Men feel they have to be good at what they do in life. If a man plays a game he feels he must win. When Jimmy Carter was president he played baseball with the press corps. The competition was intense. President Carter really wanted to win. Eunice Shriver said of her brother, John Kennedy, that he hated to lose at anything. In fact, "The only thing Jack ever got emotional about was losing."

Parents often compare the personal achievements of their sons with the accomplishments of other boys. A boy learns that other boys, and later other men, are his competitors and, therefore, potential enemies. This kind of thinking also works to undermine the development of close relationships between men.

Competition is very highly respected among men. Vince Lombardi, the great Green Bay football coach used to say, "Winning isn't everything; it's the only thing." Many coaches as well as corporation executives have held to the belief that nice guys finish last. Bobby Knight, the basketball coach at Indiana, has been criticized for his motivating by fear, his swearing, yelling and general undisciplined behavior. Many came to his defense with the simple statement, "But he wins and that's what is important." Therefore, the end justifies the means. If you can win, all else is forgiven. Winning becomes all-important.

Men generally find it difficult simply to have fun. It's hard to set aside the burden of the need to win. I must confess that I find it difficult to enjoy a game of tennis unless I win. If I lose I can actually become angry—not with my competition necessarily, but rather with my poor performance.

Of course there's nothing wrong with friendly competition, but men are so uptight about doing well and beating the competition that they often miss out on the joy of participation and the simple fun of being with friends. If they are not good at a sport or an activity, they avoid it. Why do we have to be good at what we do? So what if we are not the greatest athlete, singer, trombone player or whatever? The idea is to get involved in various social activities for the sheer joy of participating.

Most men will rarely admit to ignorance about a topic. To do so might leave the impression that they cannot compete, or are less than all-knowing. During my first year as a teacher I labored under the false belief that I as teacher (and as a man) should have all the answers to student questions. Luckily for me and my students I soon realized there was nothing wrong with saying, "I don't know." This freed me from the burden of putting on a front of being a walking encyclopedia. This way student and teacher could learn some things together. Kids won't let you play the all-knowing game. They'll give you a funny look or even say, "Who are you kidding?" Adults, on the other hand, simply keep a know-it-all at arm's length—and therefore friendless and lonely.

When my family was living in a suburb of Chicago we had a neighbor who tried to convey the impression that he knew virtually everything. This all-knowing attitude ran the gamut of topics. He became especially forceful with his religious and political opinions. We were expected to sit quietly at his feet and acquire wisdom. If we disagreed with him, he became rather emotional or even verbally hostile, as I quickly found out when I challenged his chauvinistic ideas. He was always correct and therefore intolerant of the ideas of others.

This man may be a caricature of the average adult male, but most men, while not as extreme as my old neighbor, nevertheless want to be in command of whatever they are doing, be it sports or a subject under discussion. An inordinately competitive spirit is a barrier to friendship.

Inability to Ask for Help

Men will rarely ask for help. It's tough for a man to admit deep personal needs or longings. We seem to be reluctant to seek help for anything from an ailing marriage to an ailing body. Men are reluctant to share problems not only with counselors but even with their own wives or families—and God forbid that they ask help from a friend!

If asked why he refuses to share, the usual response is he doesn't want to burden the family (friend) with problems. A man then appears as hard to reach, as removed or even aloof.

This resistance to admitting dependency on others in varying degrees is not limited only to the major areas of our lives. A woman attempted to give road directions to her brother-in-law during a trip to a family reunion. He refused to listen and proceeded to drive off in the wrong direction for what seemed to be at least half an hour. The lady was furious. "If you don't want to listen to me," she said, "at least stop at a gas station for directions." Finally the pressure became too much. By stopping at a filling station this otherwise normal male was admitting that he needed help. The women in the car expected to hear, "I'm sorry, I made a mistake." This, however, was too much for the man to say, so the carload of relatives drove off toward their intended destination—in silence.

Boys learn early to stand on their own two feet. "Don't count on others" or "God helps those who help themselves" are normal comments of good fatherly advice. Boys who cling too much to parents are potential sources of embarrassment. When my father was five or six years old his father took him to the end of a pier and threw him into Lake Michigan and said, "Swim." He added, "You must learn to take care of yourself." What my father learned was not to trust his dad and perhaps all men in general.

Too much self-sufficiency robs a man of his need for the support, love, and concern of friends.

Incorrect Priorities

Men often have a distorted order of priorities. Physical things are more important than relationships. Status is obtained by the acquisition of material wealth rather than, say, the number of close friends one might have. An acquaintance of mine years ago used to show disrespect for his wife's comments and attitudes by saying, "That's immaterial." It seems so strange that love, concern, emotions and relationships should receive second place to the material emphasis of so many men.

This distortion of emphasis on the material is certainly not a recent invention. The prophet Haggai, for example, warns that we are more concerned about living in paneled houses (material) than we are about our relationship with God and our fellow man (immaterial). (See Haggai 1:3-11.)

A man's success is measured by how much wealth and power can be acquired. Divorced men will speak with little shame when talking about their failures at home, but in sharp contrast are quite defensive if they fail in the business world. At a businessmen's lunch a man said, "I have spent the last 30 years reaching the top rung of the world's ladder of success. I now feel in my heart I was for all those years on the wrong ladder." Life had passed him by. Sure he had money but the wealth was acquired at the expense of intimacy with and the affection of his family and friends.

Unfortunately, this problem of friendlessness exists even in our churches. Larry Richards says that in church we sit together and sing together and greet one another cheerily as we leave at the end of a service. We do all of these things, sometimes for years, without forming any real personal Christian relationships. Our words often seem superficial. The church, therefore, becomes a place where Christians live alone together.

I know a man who is dying of a rare disease. His name appears in the church bulletin under the heading "Remember in Prayer." The deaconnesses send him flowers and periodically someone, usually the pastor, will offer a public prayer on his behalf. But to my knowledge, few if any men in the church have gone to spend time with him, to talk to him and to listen and to share—in short, to be his friend. The Scripture teaches us that, as we have opportunity, we are to do good unto all men (Gal. 6:10); however, we insulate ourselves from the well and the sick alike.

Men simply fear getting involved with others beyond

a superficial level. This lack of intimacy is foreign to the Scripture command to "carry each other's burdens, and in this way you will fulfill the law of Christ" (Gal. 6:2). You can't do this by keeping others at arm's length. The Galatian letter (3:27-29) reminds us that we are to enjoy fellowship together, a oneness as believers in Christ. The barriers that separate us should be destroyed.

But the barriers that separate men remain, and may even be becoming more formidable. Men pay a heavy price for their unwillingness and/or inability to remove the barriers which separate them and, therefore, prevent the formation of friendships. To be a man, a "real" man, we tend to believe that:

He shall not cry.
He shall not display weakness.
He shall not need affection or gentleness or warmth.
He shall comfort but not desire comforting.
He shall be needed but not need.
He shall touch but not be touched.
He shall be steel not flesh.
He shall be inviolate in his manhood.
He shall stand alone.[1]

Discussion Questions

1. How do you evaluate the quality of relationships which you personally have with other men?

2. List some reasons, mentioned in the chapter, that tend to prevent men from reaching out to other men for close fellowship. Discuss ways that each might be eliminated or overcome.

3. Discuss the positive and negative attributes of a life-style based on competition.

4. Why is it that men tend to measure the worth of other men on the basis of their wealth, power and physical strength? What will it take to change this?

Chapter 2

The High Cost of Being Male

"We have met the enemy and he is us." *Pogo*

Modern masculine men are prepared mentally to slug it out alone with a saber-toothed tiger but are often unfit to meet the constraints required in contemporary modern society. We are an anachronism. We learn early in life to be combative or at least competitive, yet few of us learn to be conciliatory. Few of us value close interpersonal relationships and fewer still seem willing to invest the time and emotional energy necessary for the development of closeness. The fragmentation of community life, corporate pressures, the breakdown of the extended and even the nuclear family, the drive for success, and the rate of mobility have all taken a tremendous toll on the numbers of intimate friendships we acquire and sustain.

How has all this affected our quality of life?

By the traditional retirement age of 65 there are only 75 men alive for every 100 women. It may be an exaggeration to conclude that men are slowly killing themselves, but the grim facts are nevertheless quite frightening. Women on the average live a full seven years longer than men. Life-span projections for baby girls born in the early 1980s has now reached 80 years. For baby boys the projection is about 73 years.

If the forecast of an earlier grave is not bad enough, there is more bad news. The fortunate men who do remain alive into old age tend to have more physical problems than women. In the book *The Total Man*, Dan Benson reports that in marriages where both are still living one of the pair is an invalid—and it is usually the husband. The onetime strong, independent, competitive man must be cared for by a healthy wife. Benson believes that men who are unable to express emotions or to seek help in time of need or to show gentleness and caring, finally, after many years, pay a very heavy price physically.[2]

The way we think and act reduces not only the quantity of life but also its quality. This is a staggering proposition which certainly needs our attention.

Stress: Positive or Negative?

It was during the mid 1930s that Dr. Hans Selye first discovered the terrible effects that stress has upon the human body. His work with hormones and the endocrine glands revealed a strong correlation between the way the mind and body function. If you are friendless, lonely, working under great pressures, frustrated, or in other ways maladjusted mentally over a long period of time, you create wear and tear on your body as well as your mind. Psychosomatic disorders—those diseases or ailments that have their origin in your mind—are physically real and can have a devastating impact upon both the quality and the length of your life.

As dangerous as stress can be, we need not fear the

frequent pressure-packed moments of everyday living that so often create stress. Stressful experiences are a normal part of a man's social and work life. The available research suggests that it is not so much the amount of stress one experiences that affects mental and physical health but rather the manner in which one handles the stress. If your boss is difficult to work for, this is sure to produce anxiety and stress, but it doesn't have to affect your health or feelings of self-worth.

Many researchers argue that the key to harmlessly venting daily stress is a strong network of friends and family. Breaking ties, as in divorce for example, or never having established such relationships, appears to increase the incidence of heart disease, strokes, hypertension, migraine and tension headaches, rashes, ulcers, and even infectious diseases such as tuberculosis. If we are to avoid their potentially ruinous impact we must share the frustration, stresses, loneliness, and anxieties of everyday life with people we love and who love us in return.

Physicians Meyer Friedman and Ray H. Rosenman in their book *Type A Behavior and Your Heart* list numerous behavioral characteristics that appear in high-risk heart patients. They include a sense of time urgency, a persistent desire for recognition and advancement, a strong competitive drive, an emphasis on work at the expense of social and family life, and a tendency to take on excessive responsibilities because of the feeling that "only I can do it."

Take notice that these damaging traits are usually associated with men rather than women. Read over the list again. These traits are almost synonymous with what we have learned to believe is male behavior. It is how we respond to stress rather than the stress itself that gives us our problems. Women experience stress too, as Helen A. DeRosis points out in her book *Women and Anxiety*. Yet, not having to live up to the same unrealistic expectations, women adapt to stress and other problems better than men.

A study conducted by the University of California at Berkeley has shown that American men are among those who have the highest heart disease rates in the entire world. Japanese men, for example, have a much lower rate of coronary disease. Such variables as diet, smoking, and drinking were not as important as life-style. Japan is a highly industrialized society with a dense population living within a relatively small archipelago. There are approximately 125 million Japanese living in an area the size of California. But while tension and stress are present, emphasis is upon the importance of family and friends. Because of their priorities they are able to defuse the stresses inherent in many industrialized jobs.

It has been my privilege to meet and act as host to several Japanese teachers and administrators who were visiting the United States. I was impressed with their orientation towards family and friends. Americans tend to think in an "I" or "me" context while Japanese seem to support a "we" mind set. The Japanese seem more likely to view themselves as part of a group than as autonomous individuals. They are responsible to others and in harmony with others. In contrast, Americans strive for freedom and independence.

In the longevity game it is the men who lead balanced lives who win. They mix work with fun. People who live long, happy lives are not one-dimensional. University of Wisconsin expert on aging, Dr. Roger J. Samp, says that these people have learned to pace their lives. "They were responsive and appreciative of the world around them. They liked simple things like flowers, dogs, and northern lights, and they were able to enjoy the traffic along a detour instead of cussing the highway department."[3]

Job: Blessing or Barrier

Jack Houston, careers editor for the *Chicago Tribune*, argues that too often a job puts American men in a position of having to choose between their jobs and their friends, spouse, or family. This statement is largely spurious. If a man is forced to choose, as Houston claims, then the job is demanding more time and energy than should be either expected or provided. Men can't blame their jobs for their lack of close friendships or close family ties. I think that jobs which are extremely demanding and consume most of a man's energy and time are rare. And men who do work in these positions usually do so of their own free will.

A 55-year-old head mechanic for a large cement company works approximately 80 hours a week. His job and his life are inseparable. He has allowed the job to become not only his principal interest, but his only real concern in life. His wife and children rarely see him. He never visits his mother or siblings, even though they live in the same suburban area. He doesn't need the money the extra hours produce. His boss would be just as happy if the man worked a normal 40 hours. The man's life consists of working, and in the few remaining hours, sitting in front of the television. Subconsciously he avoids the possibility of intimacy at every turn. He uses his job as a barrier, preventing others from reaching out to him. His obsession with work ruined his first marriage and has sapped the vitality from the second. He has no friends and his own children have walked out of his life following years of neglect and rejection.

Dr. John M. Rhoads of Duke University concludes from research that those who spend an inordinate amount of attention to their jobs have few outside interests, little sense of humor, rarely take vacations, and worry about problems when it is inappropriate to do so.

While the Bible warns us about the sin of laziness, it also warns us about work that is unnecessarily demanding: "It is in vain that you rise up early and go late to rest, eating the bread of anxious toil; for he gives to his beloved sleep" (Ps. 127:2, *RSV*).

Our culture teaches us that our performance in the work place leads to money, status and even power. Richard Huber, in his book *The American Idea of Success*, says that success is not learned by being a loyal friend or a good husband. Rather it is a reward for performance on the job. Acquiring and enjoying material wealth is a pursuit worthy of our attention and is justified in such varied sources as the Bible and Adam Smith, author of early capitalist theory. My point here is not to challenge our desire to acquire wealth. My concern rather is with a preoccupation with this aspect of life.

At work, if we're busy or in some way unavailable, this is supposed to translate into being important and responsible. Yet it is the man who allows himself to become overworked who tends to be the least effective. He's hampered by incidentals. He finds it difficult to say no to virtually any request and therefore may not perform well at any task. If you feel you're not a workaholic but that the company is simply demanding more of your time than is justified, it may be time to look for another job. The book *What Color Is Your Parachute?*, by Richard N. Bolles, will get you started looking for new employment.

Despite the pressures to perform well in the work place, the real problem lies elsewhere. If your job truly prevents you from leading a balanced life you'll need to make a change if possible. If, in your judgment, you are too old to change jobs, or are locked into a pension plan, perhaps you can change departments or responsibilities without leaving your present employer. Don't cling to a rotten job just because it seems secure.

The Real Problem

For most of us, our problem is not with our jobs but rather with ourselves. No it is not our job that contributes to the calamity of our friendless condition or our psychosomatic disorders, but rather how we view ourselves, and how we think and behave, that get us into trouble. We have learned to withstand and keep to ourselves pain, loneliness, fear and anything else that has a taint of humanness. Indeed we believe that we have to withstand feelings, and have been so taught. Denying our feelings or sense experience will work to produce psychosomatic disorders and may lead us to early graves.

If we fail to obtain the required level of insensitivity and strength—the plight of most of us mortals—that failure is likely to produce frustrations and a sense that we are somehow less a man. Someone once wrote that the birthright of every American male is a chronic sense of personal inadequacy. The problem is not with our failure to reach the standard but rather with the standard itself.

Dan Benson believes that "the American masculine dream is killing us."[4] This unobtainable dream or standard is, according to Benson, the Spanish machismo concept of a man being an unswerving pinnacle of strength. This is the nonemotional creature that takes on all tasks and problems with unfaltering success.

If we repress our emotions do they disappear? Hardly. Denial and repression force our emotions to be revealed in some distorted fashion either mentally or physically. There is not a man who has been born who does not have a basic need for emotional release. We're unable to survive without it. Wagenvoord believes that "a man is never able to completely suppress his inner self. He can hide it, or rationalize it, or diminish its importance, but he isn't able to banish that self permanently. Of course, the continual struggle between what he wants and what he thinks is required of him makes his emotions erupt in fits and starts. A brief explosion of inexplicable tears, an outburst of sudden affection, a late-night confidence—these are the humanizing cracks in his mask."[5]

Men seem to falter in their relationships with others partially because they mentally live in a world that no longer exists. For hundreds of years, and in most cultures, persistent human needs were largely material. The principal concern of people was survival. Acquiring the basic material necessities of life was a full-time job. Men had little time to do anything but work hard. The emphasis upon survival was altered for most men living in the Western world following the widespread influence of the industrial revolution in the mid-eighteenth century. With advancements in farming and science the average working man, regardless of his social class, has spent fewer hours acquiring the essentials for biological survival.

Technology changes faster than attitudes and human behavior, however. People may resist change or, without much thought, follow old outmoded patterns of behavior. Many resist positive change with the exhortation, "But we've never done it that way before."

Despite the removal of the threat of hunger or starvation in the Western nations, many among our species still concentrate all of their energies acquiring material wealth as if somehow their very physical survival depends on it. Too much attention is devoted to physical needs at the expense of what might be referred to as psycho/spiritual needs. When survival needs are satisfied, these other needs surface and also must be satisfied. If neglected, as is the case with most American men, we will see distorted personalities in varying degrees.

Abraham H. Maslow, the psychologist who has done

a great deal to advance our understanding of human motivation, argues that once basic physical needs are met we are then free to concern ourselves with deeper, more advanced levels of human needs. Maslow argues that the physiological needs of hunger, thirst and air are of obvious and utmost importance. Once these are satisfied we are motivated to free ourselves from physical threat or dangers. We are captivated by our efforts to obtain a secure physical environment.

But even with a safe and secure physical and material world well in hand, many men continue to work as if the wolf were still at the door. Columnist Sydney J. Harris mentions that the "success" books rarely emphasize that the same qualities which take you to the top can also drop you to the bottom. Personality traits don't exist in a vacuum. What may be a virtue or help in one situation or time period might well be a detriment in another. Holding in high esteem the values of power, materialism, and status may have served men better in years gone by than today. Achieving bodily comforts and positions of power and prestige does not in itself satisfy, over the long haul, the longings of the human spirit.

What is it that is lacking? Just what are our basic emotional soul needs? Psychologists, sociologists and theologians have studied this question for decades. In the early part of this century, sociologist William Thomas worked on this question, as have Louis Raths and Anna Burrell and other scientists more recently. The findings are similar: all humans have five major emotional needs that must be satisfied if they are to function as well-adjusted happy individuals. The person who has met these core needs is at peace with himself and his world and is a contributing member of his society. To reach this state of mind a person must possess the following in ample supply.

Belonging and Love

Each of us needs to feel that we are an important part of a whole. We all suffer from an enormous fear of being rejected. The need for recognition or belonging is the need to feel worthwhile. Having the knowledge that one is accepted and even loved by others provides us with emotional security. Whether we admit it or not, we also need to belong to and be accepted by God. The ultimate expression of belonging is knowing that we are created by a personal God who loves us. We have worth and dignity not because of what we can do or produce but because we are a created being of Almighty God.

Several decades ago a study was conducted within a South American orphanage. Normal physical care was provided the babies, but because the orphanage was so badly understaffed, the overworked nurses were unable to play with or show affection to the children. The babies responded at first by crying. Later they lost their appetites, became restless and nervous. More than 90 babies became ill or died solely due to a lack of love. Approximately 20 children survived but were hopelessly mentally ill as they grew older.

None of us can function without others. We need the love and affection of other people throughout life.

Accomplishment

Goals, both short- and long-term, are important to our mental health. People who feel they are not accomplishing all they should in life usually think of themselves as failures. Men need to anticipate, to work for the successful conclusion of projects large and small.

One of the secrets of longevity is to continue to plan and anticipate. A common trait of those who live in good health to a ripe old age is the ability to live for tomorrow. In Maslow's theory the accomplishment need is referred to as *self-actualization*, or the ongoing need to improve.

Meeting this basic need provides a sense of meaning and significance to a man's life. Many are able to meet this basic need via a job, church, or some form of public service. In short, we need to feel that what we do in life is important.

Freedom from Emotional Fear and Guilt

Regret about how we occasionally behave and think is normal. But some become so obsessed and handicapped with guilt that they almost fail to function. Fear and even guilt should be experienced, but in non-crippling doses. Fear can help us protect ourselves or motivate us to do what we should. Dr. Karl Menninger, in his excellent book *Whatever Became of Sin?*, argues that we need certain forms of fear and guilt to help motivate us to do what is right. But it is the negative, unconscious fears that can cripple the expressions of personality.

In speaking of _____, irrational fears, psychologist Sol Gordon says, "They distort reality, create illusions, and destroy our capacity to deal with the outside world." On the most simple and literal level it can be demonstrated that a person who is intensely afraid can't even recognize a straight line as being straight.[6]

There are people who show an exaggerated, unmotivated sense of apprehension in regard to most of the experiences of life. They seem almost literally to be afraid of everything. Such people are unsure of their own abilities. It is from these false fears and guilts that we need freedom. To obtain this freedom requires a healthy attitude about one's self-worth and abilities.

Self-Respect

We need to feel good about ourselves. Self-confidence and self-respect are prerequisites for a meaningful life. Our feelings about ourselves are developed during relationships with other people. This is not self-preoccupation or narcissism. You must feel good about yourself or you'll be incapacitated emotionally. Remember the Scripture says to "love your neighbor as yourself" (Mark 12:31). John Powell, author of *The Secret of Staying in Love*, argues that all psychological problems, from a mild neurosis to the deepest psychosis, are symptomatic of the frustration of this fundamental human need for a healthy sense of self-respect.

Understanding

This is a two-sided basic human need. Each individual needs to feel that his attitudes, beliefs, and ideas are understood by others. We need people to understand us. Conversely we need to experience and understand deeply the attitudes and feelings others possess. To accomplish this interaction requires in-depth communication where empathy is expressed.

Are these five needs met sufficiently in your own life? Or do you suffer in mind, body, and spirit because of sundry stresses, unrealistic expectations, loneliness, and distorted priorities?

In a do-it-yourself mental health checkup the famous Menninger Foundation men are provided the opportunity to evaluate if serious problems exist in their own lives. Ask yourself the same checkup questions:

1. What are my goals in life and how realistic are they?

2. Is my use of time and energy helping me to reach these goals?

3. Do I have a proper sense of responsibility or do I try to do too much and fail to acknowledge my limitations?

4. How do I react to disappointments and losses?

5. How am I coping with stress and anxiety?

6. What is the consistency and quality of my personal relationships? Are my contacts with others superficial, meager, and unrewarding?

7. From whom do I receive and to whom do I give emotional support? Do I avoid getting support from others for fear of appearing weak?

8. What is the role of love in my life? How much time do I give to listen to and care for others? (From a copyrighted article in *U.S. News and World Report* of May 10, 1976.)

Note questions 6,7 and 8. Your answers to these questions alone should give you some idea as to the quality of interpersonal relationships you have with others. Most men do not score very well, especially on the last three questions. Our interpersonal relationships tend to be anemic. We must free ourselves from the social and psychological constraints which we have learned and which now prevent us from meeting our God-given basic needs. If we are honest about our condition, that is if we admit to ourselves that our relationships with others are not what they should be, then we can begin to make corrections.

Discussion Questions

1. Why is a strong network of family and friendships essential to both the quality and quantity of life?

2. How have we as men carried the value of self-reliance to a distorted extreme? How can we change this situation?

3. Do you agree that aspects of your behavior and attitudes may actually affect the length of your life? What are the implications of this for you?

4. Take the do-it-yourself Menninger mental health checkup. How did you score? Discuss the test and your responses with another person.

Chapter 3
What's the Difference?

"Male and female he created them." *Genesis 1:27*

Women are different from men—and God wanted it that way. God deliberately created both male and female.

Women make friends easier than men. They form and sustain relationships at a more qualitative level than do men. Psychologist Elaine Sachnoff concludes from research that friendship means more to women than to men. Their relationships tend to be more meaningful, satisfying and last longer.

The two assumptions—(1) that the sexes differ, and (2) that women have more satisfying friendships than men—are truths that require little elaboration. But here the agreement ends. The difficult questions we need to face are (1) how do the sexes differ, and (2) does "maleness" or "femaleness" affect the making and nurturing of relationships with other humans? Do the differences affect our ability to form friendships? Can we as men blame sex differences for our friendless condition? Must "maleness" somehow hinder a man from forming and encouraging close relationships with other men? The explorations of these questions will help us better understand both our limitations and our potentials as men.

Sexual differences are facts of nature which cannot be minimized or ignored. Many are too obvious to even mention. Much of the recent research dealing with the sexes has been conducted to attempt to prove that females are not inferior to males. Therefore, there has been a distinct tendency to minimize the differences both in scientific and popular literature.

Physical Differences

Despite the claims of some people, the sexes really are different. In a survey of the literature on sex differences, Dr. David McClelland of Harvard concludes that literally thousands of studies show that significant sex differences do indeed exist. In all human societies men are larger and stronger than women. The average man is 6 percent taller than the average woman. Also men average about 20 percent more weight than women. This is caused by greater body bulk, mainly from larger muscles and bones. Large muscles in males permit them to lift more weight, throw a ball farther or run faster than most women. Even at birth the male has more strength to lift his head higher and for longer periods of time than do females. At puberty the difference in muscle strength is accentuated, largely due to testosterone.

Men have a higher metabolic rate and produce more physical energy than women and thus need more food to keep the body performing to its full potential. Women are usually a few degrees cooler than men, and may therefore require less food to maintain a constant weight. Men's blood is richer than women's with an average of 300,000 more red corpuscles per cubic millimeter.

With statistics like these it's understandable why many

have concluded that men are physically superior to women. Even some scientists who should know better have fallen for the male superiority myth. Not too surprisingly most of these scientists have been men. For example, Lester Ward, a founding father of American sociology, stated a few decades ago that women were cautious and more conservative than men because of their biological helplessness. Statements of this kind undermine the objective, value-free image that contemporary sociologists want to convey. Scientists in more recent years are less willing to so blatantly express their theories.

Recent research has confirmed, however, that rather than being inferior physically, women actually possess certain biological advantages when compared with men. Dr. Estelle Ramey, an endocrinologist of Georgetown University School of Medicine, believes that women outlive men because they are biologically stronger, not because they lead lives that are less stressful. This generalization fails to consider the ways American men live their lives that we discussed in chapters 1 and 2. Nevertheless there are some apparent real physical advantages that females enjoy.

Biological differences are established at conception. It's estimated that between 130 and 150 males are conceived for every 100 females. Conception is probably men's only fundamental biological advantage. But after this beginning of human life, it's downhill for the male sex. Scientists say that by the time of birth, there are only 106 boys to every 100 girls. Many more male fetuses are lost to miscarriages because of spontaneous abortion and death in utero.

The United States Bureau of Vital Statistics estimates that 25 percent more boy babies than girl babies are born prematurely. Circulatory and respiratory infection, parasites, and viral and digestive diseases plague boys in higher numbers than girls. In fact, there is rarely a disease or defect which doesn't wield its damage more in boys than in girls.

During the first year of life the mortality rate among boys is almost one-third higher than among girls. Boys have more genetic defects which contribute to the higher death rate. And as if that was not enough, the sobering news continues. The female physical advantage goes on throughout life into old age.

Men and women differ in every cell of their bodies. In the nucleus of each body's millions of cells there is present either an XX chromosome for women or an XY chromosome for men. For centuries husbands have placed on their wives the burden of producing a healthy boy baby. And yet the genetic fact is that, if a baby is to be a boy, the father must come up with the Y chromosome, the primary sex determiner.

Each female cell contains the chromatin substance that is absent in male cells. To date the purpose of chromatin is unknown. The male nervous system too is different from women's, as are other parts of his body. The characteristics listed here, and countless others as well, show that there are real biological differences within our species. This research reflects the truth of Scripture which says that God created humans distinctly as male and female. "God created man in his own image, in the image of God he created him; male and female he created them" (Gen. 1:27).

Psychological Differences

If the sexes are different physically aren't they also different psychologically? And if they are indeed different mentally, how much of a difference really exists? Unless we are able to believe that mind and body are completely separate realms, we should expect psychological as well as the more obvious physical differences between the sexes. As you might imagine, this topic is fraught with controversy and confusion which will not be resolved in this brief discussion.

People tend to line up at one extreme or the other on this psychological issue as they do when the issue is biology. One group claims that men and women are totally different mentally. For example, they point out that women are religious, men are not; women are gentle, men are rough; men are independent, women need security; women talk a great deal, while men talk very little; women appreciate the arts and literature, men do not; women need to care for children, men do not; men need goals and accomplishments, women do not. And the list of stereotypes goes on.

This group maintains that heredity makes men and women completely different not only physically but also in the way we think and behave. Many of the men who hold this view are chauvinists who have acquired a stereotype of "what women are like." Some chauvinists are also playboys who view women as possessions or solely as objects of pleasure. The playboy mentality maintains that the ideal woman has a small brain and large breasts. Chauvinists can also be well-meaning Christians or even pastors who adhere to a limited view of the sexes.

There are many popular books and sermons dealing with family living. We often learn of *the* role of men and *the* role of women. For example, many people emphasize that the Bible says wives should "submit to" their husbands (Eph. 5:22). But did you know that the Scripture also demands that husbands submit to their wives? Well it does. Back up a verse from the frequently cited Ephesians 5:22 and you find, "Submit to one another out of reverence for Christ" (Eph. 5:21). Submission is not for wives only. We rarely hear this fact because we are locked into a culture that does not view submission as a manly trait.

At the other extreme, there are those who contend that there really are no psychological or mental differences between the sexes. Men and women have the same abilities and each will perform or behave in exactly the same fashion if given both the chance and the same early formal and informal educational experiences. Many feminists maintain the view that all differences are culturally determined and have nothing to do with heredity. They say that you act like a woman not because you are a woman but because you were taught to act in a certain fashion by parents, teachers, and society.

In the 1930s Dr. Margaret Mead studied the differences in male and female behavior in three tribes of New Guinea. She argued that sex roles are different in different areas of the world, and thus concluded that we have no basis for linking one's sex with one's behavior or attitude.[7]

I had an opportunity to talk with Dr. Mead about this topic of sex difference during an anthropology conference several years ago. Our meeting took place shortly before she died. She seemed to have changed her published views somewhat, or at least held them with less vigor. She doubted some of her earlier conclusions, believing that there might exist innate psychological differences between the sexes, but was unwilling to speculate on which traits might be either learned or innate.

Both views of the sexes—that psychological traits are completely innate or totally learned—are largely mythical. Both of these extremes need to be avoided. There really are differences, but they are not as extensive as many would like us to believe. There is substantial evidence that men and women share similar behavior and in some areas manifest different behavior. Widespread agreement exists among scientists on this. The following contains many of their agreements related to sex differences. Note that of all the hundreds of possible behaviors, only a handful are listed as either largely male or female in characteristics. Note also that the first trait is directly related to the formation of friendships.

• Women are more likely than men to express their emotions and display empathy and compassion in response to the emotions of others.

• Men as a whole are more skillful than women at visually perceiving the spatial, or geometric, features of objects. A typical test of this ability involves matching a drawing of an object with the correct drawing of the object from another angle, or as it would be if rotated in space.

• Girls score higher than boys on tests of verbal ability, such as comprehension and production of language, analogies, and spelling. Most evidence shows that this difference appears during adolescence and widens at least through high school.

• A similar developmental difference holds for mathematical abilities, except that in this case boys achieve the higher scores. This may be a result of boys' superior visual-spatial ability, a capacity useful in solving some mathematical problems.

• Females tend to be more anxious than males about risking failure. When they do fail, they are more likely to blame themselves. When males fail, they tend to blame others.

• Boys tend to be more physically active than girls, doing more running and jumping. At play, they range farther than do girls.[8]

What Is Male? What Is Female?
In 1974 Dr. Carol N. Jacklin and Dr. Eleanor E. Mac-

coby of Stanford University released a study, *The Psychology of Sex Differences*, that is now widely known and respected. They reviewed and summarized the research of over 2,000 books and articles dealing with sex differences in motivation, social behavior and intellectual ability.

Boyce Rensberger, commenting on the work of Jacklin and Maccoby, mentions that they concluded that the preponderance of evidence pointed to few areas of real difference: males have superior verbal ability, males excel at visual-spatial tasks, and males are better at math. In addition, the researchers believed that the evidence was sufficient to reject eight myths about sex differences. They concluded that the sexes do not differ in (1) sociability, (2) self-esteem, (3) motivation to achieve, (4) facility at rote learning, (5)analytic mindedness, (6) susceptibility to environmental influences, or (7) response to auditory/visual stimuli. These characteristics are not biological in nature. I know we tend to believe that our thinking is natural but in many cases it is learned.

Boyce Rensberger says, "Because the individual's own responses seem spontaneous and natural to him, he often regards them as part of his essential humanity rather than as the result of a particular training and experience. On the other hand, once the efficacy of socialization is understood, it is easy to fall into the opposite fallacy and to deny that there are limitations to human malleability."[9] The point is this: within the few God-ordained differences, there is much room for change and growth.

God has given to us, as men and women, diverse temperaments, talents, skills, and even motivations that make us unique at birth. But we must be aware that our culture clouds our understanding of what is male or what is female. For example, from the Rensberger report, while women are more likely than men to express emotions and reveal empathy and compassion, nothing exists in Scripture or science which says that this is the natural order of things. Therefore, despite our current cultural traits that teach that the expression of emotions, including compassion and empathy, are largely female traits, it doesn't have to be this way. We too as men can learn these traits.

We're capable of more diverse behavior than we might realize. For example, some of you may think that cleaning the dishes is a woman's job. This idea comes from our culture, certainly not from the Bible. In fact, 2 Kings 21:13 talks about a man wiping dishes. Certain tasks in our society such as changing diapers, mowing the lawn, grocery shopping, driving the kids to school, managing the checkbook, and housecleaning are said to be either woman's work or man's work. All of this role fixation is cultural rather than biblical.

In our home my wife and I, and recently our children too, do the housecleaning together. We call this activity "dummy time," mainly I guess because no one really wants to do it. But working together is fun and the time spent in "dummy time" is over much sooner when more than one person works at it. The point is that family members should think of others within the family when work needs to be done instead of wasting time trying to decide which job is for males and which is for females.

One man, following his wife's request that he help with the housework, remarked sarcastically, "That's not my job. The next thing I know she'll be asking me to wear dresses and use perfume and makeup. I'm a man. Doesn't she realize that?" But even with this extreme comment we can find historical illustrations when wigs, bloomers, long stockings, lace blouses and high heels were worn by men and considered manly in the time period in which they appeared. During our own colonial period many of these items were popular with men.

The columnist Sydney Harris expresses his irritation with our culture's narrow and distorted definition of what is manliness in the following story:

As I was edging out of a parking lot the other day, some Clyde in his Bonneville cut sharply ahead of me, flashed a sour smile of triumph in my direction and scooted away. He thought he was displaying strength and aggressiveness; I thought he was displaying weakness and bad manners.

What the prevailing ethos in modern American life does not seem to understand is that true strength always reveals itself in gentleness and courtesy; this was the whole medieval idea of knighthood and chivalry—a knight was chivalrous because he felt strong enough to afford it.

We tend to confuse rudeness with power and aggressiveness with virility. Many, if not most, of the bad-mannered drivers on the road are slack-jawed youths who privately feel weak and insecure in their personal relations with the world; tooling a ferocious car gives them a vicarious sense of power they do not possess in person.

Genuine strength of character is always accompanied by a feeling of security that allows one to practice civility and courtesy—but, in our perverse culture, civility and courtesy are often regarded as signs of weakness or some lack of "manliness."

And it is largely this perverse evaluation of what constitutes manhood that accounts for so much of the dangerous discourtesy on our nation's highways—somehow, the education of boys here has stressed aggressiveness at the price of gentleness, so that many youths act like boors in order to be thought of as "men."

This is fairly indigenous to our culture; in other countries, a more balanced view is taken of what comprises "manliness," and one of the main criteria of an adult male is his considerateness for others. And the poor result of our misconception of manhood can be seen in many failing marriages, where the wives uniformly complain that their husbands are just "little boys who failed to grow up."[10]

Our definition of manliness or masculinity is too narrow and usually distorted. We see ourselves and women as opposites; we even use the phrase "the opposite sex." But we're not opposite; we are different. Remember, of the 48 chromosomes in each human cell only one relates to sex.

In the Eyes of God

Throughout history, most people, including Christians, have assumed that a proper interpretation of Genesis 1:27 meant that any and all differences in their society between males and females existed because God created these differences, not because they had learned them within their culture.

With the emergence of the social and behavioral sciences we have begun to question the "absolute role" which physiology plays in the formation of sexual temperament and behavior. Through cross-cultural research, social scientists now surmise that "culture," rather than "nature," is the major influence in determining the temperamental differences between the sexes. In other words we are more alike than we previously realized. Following the Great Depression women began in large numbers to enter the work force and by the early 1980s one woman in every two was working outside the home. And men today are more likely to help with children and domestic tasks that historically have been considered woman's work. So much for the Ozzie and Harriet or *Father Knows Best* stereotype of the husband as sole provider and the wife as the nonemployed partner who cares for the kids and prepares meals.

It is incorrect for Christians to assume that their particular definition of masculinity and femininity learned in their culture is God's definition. There exists an arrogance in holders to this ethnocentric view of the world. We fall into this trap by reading our cultural expectations into Scripture. When the Scripture comments on basic human traits it doesn't distinguish between the sexes. Therefore, for example, in the Sermon on the Mount the Lord calls those blessed who are sorrowful, who possess a gentle spirit, who show mercy, whose hearts are pure, and who are peaceful.

While some are incorrect in defining sex roles and behavior too narrowly, it is important that we don't go to the other extreme. We are neither opposite nor the same. We as men and women are different. We all know we're different, but some have been trapped into forgetting it by the cry for equality between the sexes. Equality is plainly the wrong word. Red is not "equal" to blue, and a pear is not "equal" to an apple. Unless we are talking about an equality of merit or worth the term does not apply. Of course men and women are equal in this sense, but that is not where the discussion seems to be in our society.

Some say today, "I am a person, not a man or woman." The unisex view goes against the grain of history. Despite the arguments of a vocal minority, there are real biological and psychological differences. Androgyny is neither biblical nor scientific. Thomas Howard, professor of English at Gordon College, says that throughout history in all tribes and cultures, people have recognized sexual differences and have seen them not as horrid but as blissful. The stark biological distinctions attest to the overwhelming and basic fact that men and women are indeed different. So while it is to our benefit to broaden our definition of what it is to be a man we don't, in the process, want to destroy the distinctions between the sexes.

Jack Balswick, a Ph.D. in sociology, argues that the strongest evidence that innate temperamental differences exist with each sex is the general similarity of behavior for males and females in most cultures. While the sexes differ in physiology and in temperament, much of what we call male or female behavior or attitudes is social conditioning (nurture) rather than the result of biology (nature). Much behavior that is now explained as biologically either male or female may just as easily be explained by social conditioning.

This is good news. You're more malleable than you may have realized. Sure you're a man, but that doesn't mean you cannot learn to be a compassionate, courteous, loving, listening, caring human being if you're now lacking any of these characteristics. The point is, *if you don't have the traits that develop friendships, you can acquire them.*

Dr. Robert Bell, a professor of sociology at Temple University, is of the opinion that it is pseudo-scientific to argue that women are genetically programmed differently from men in friendship possibilities. You're not locked into your male bigotry in a narrow sense. If women acquire and maintain friendships better than men—and they do—men are free to acquire the characteristics that women possess.

I have no intention of minimizing the distinctions that

God makes between the sexes. They are real and they are good. But we must remember that we as men and women are more alike than we realize. So if you're caught in some limited male role that you have attributed to your maleness, you need to realize that your behavior may actually be the result of social learning rather than your biological or temperamental maleness.

How can you determine if an aspect of your personality is the product of nature or just social conditioning? Use the following test. Ask yourself: Is this aspect of my personality a positive attribute or is it destructive? If it is destructive, you can bet that God didn't make you that way (nature). The behavior was learned (nurture). If a certain behavior hinders the formation of friendships it should be viewed not as masculine but as destructive. If behavior encourages friendship formation, view this behavior as positive.

The great thing about learned negative behavior is that you can unlearn it and thus gain a fresh start. There's a story about a woman who for years cut off both ends of a ham before cooking it. Her inquisitive daughter asked, "Why do you cut off each end, Mom?" The response, "I don't really know. I've always done it that way. I guess I learned it from your grandmother." Undaunted the little girl asked her grandmother why both she and Mother "cut off the ends." Grandmother was surprised to learn that this had become a family tradition. "Honey," she said, "I had to cut off the ends because the ham wouldn't fit in my small roasting pan."

You may laugh at this story but don't miss its message. We have learned many things in life, and what we have learned contributes to the current way we now live our lives. Some of what we have learned, like the lady who still hacks off the ends of the ham, is unnecessary but harmless. We have also acquired, from earlier learning, much that is positive and good. But there exist aspects of our early training that are cultural baggage which we should dispose of. Much of this destructive learning results because of a narrow and incorrect view of what constitutes manliness.

Our God-given maleness need not be a social handicap and should not be used by us to defend a friendless existence. A man told me, "Of course I don't have friends. I'm a man. My wife is the one with the friends." His implication was that his friendless condition was part of his genetic rather than his social background. Our biological "maleness" is not a barrier to developing relationships, and social barriers can be unlearned. We have no excuses other than our own resistance to change. This alone prevents us from cultivating the warm, meaningful relationships enjoyed by many women and only a handful of other men.

Discussion Questions

1. Do you believe that being a man should in any way affect your ability to make quality friendships? Why? Why not?

2. In what ways has our culture provided definitions of what it means to be male that are in conflict with either the Bible or scientific research?

3. We use the term "opposite sex." What other terms would be more accurate?

4. What aspects of your personality are destructive that you can change through prayer and commitment?

Chapter 4

Biblical Principles of Friendship

"You have made known to me the path of life."
Psalm 16:11

Friendships are desired by each of us. But many may not recognize the true nature of friendship, mistaking it for various counterfeits. Fortunately the Bible offers examples and principles for us to learn from and to apply to our own lives.

Perhaps the greatest biblical example of two men in close fellowship is the relationship between David and Jonathan. Their unity is mentioned in 1 Samuel 18:1, "The soul of Jonathan was knit to the soul of David" (*RSV*).

Jonathan was the oldest son of Saul who was the first king of the nation of Israel. Jonathan had many great military victories over various enemies of Israel, but he is remembered not so much for his military wisdom and bravery but rather as the friend of David. David became Israel's greatest king and one of the most important individuals in all of the Old Testament.

The two men met shortly after David's successful encounter with the Philistine, Goliath. David and Jonathan's love for each other began the day they met and continued over time, despite social class differences. Jonathan's father was also a problem for the friendship in that he tried on several occasions to kill David. Jonathan more than once risked his own life for David. On one occasion Saul was angry because Jonathan did not hold his hostile view of David. Saul, unable to control his emotions, actually threw a spear at his own son. Despite the unpredictable harassment and danger, Jonathan remained committed to his friend, David. David too, despite the inherent dangers of secretly meeting with the king's son, remained loyal to Jonathan.

For a biblical example of what not to do in a friendship we need to turn to what is probably the oldest book in the Bible—the book of Job. This great section of Scripture illustrates that, despite circumstances, man has the capacity for a faith completely centered on God.

Job's multiple sufferings were compounded not just with a lack of sympathy but with an actual overt emotional harassment and condemnation by his three so-called friends. Zophar, Eliphaz and Bildad told Job he must have committed some gross sin. Why else would he be suffering so much, they reasoned.

Eliphaz summed up their thinking (4:7,8) when he asked Job a rhetorical question: "Consider now: Who, being innocent, has ever perished? Where were the upright ever destroyed?" Eliphaz continues without waiting for Job's response. "As I have observed, those who plow evil and those who sow trouble reap it." You can almost feel the judgmental and self-righteous tone of this man's voice as you read the passage.

The fact is, these pseudo-friends with their criticism and self-righteousness, failed to see the whole of Job's situation. They wouldn't even try to look at Job's pain from a different point of view. They reached the easy but wrong conclusion that God must be punishing Job for some unrevealed sin.

When we compare the relationship between David and Jonathan with that of Job and Eliphaz and crew, we would all prefer the kindness and affection of David and Jonathan.

But close friendships don't just happen. They result from the application of principles recorded throughout the Word of God.

While preparing to write this book I read through the Bible with the specific purpose of finding rules or principles on the doctrine of friendship. I was at first surprised to learn that God has so much to say about this topic. We tend to think of the Bible as a book of redemption, which is true, but the Bible also includes a great deal about our relationships with other people. In fact, the Bible touches upon every kind of human relationship, including friendship.

The Bible places emphasis upon six principles of friendship. These are basic themes which keep appearing in different examples throughout Scripture. In the following survey of these six principles we will learn what spiritual and/or personality traits need to be either added or deleted for our personal lives.

Principle #1: God-Centered

When two men share the same core values which are focused upon Christ, they are free to allow their relationship to grow. The Christian believes, today as the Westminster Shorter Catechism recorded in 1793, that "man's chief end is to glorify God and to enjoy Him forever." Intimate friendships rarely develop when individuals do not share at least a basic consensus of beliefs.

With the same biblical value system two men can seek each other's counsel and can have confidence that the responses will be based on Scripture. David, for example, came to Jonathan for counsel (1 Sam. 20) knowing the advice would be sound. Moses accepted the advice of Jethro, as Timothy did of Paul.

In Psalm 1:1 we learn that "blessed is the man who does not walk in the counsel of the wicked." In 2 Corinthians 6:14 we read, "Do not be yoked together with unbelievers." Nowhere in Scripture do we find close friendships without the unifying force of a common faith in God.

Principle #2: Formation of Covenant

"And Jonathan made a covenant with David because he loved him as himself" (1 Sam. 18:3).

Virtually every important relationship or event in our society is acknowledged with ritual and ceremony and witnessed by people. Marriage is the best illustration of this. The couple is formally recognized by relatives, friends, the church, and even by the legal structure. Recognition takes the form of what anthropologists call "rites of passage." Rites occur at birth, baptism, graduation, in club memberships, and at death. These and other transitions are accompanied by some formal ritual that signifies the passing from one stage of life into another. Through ceremony we recognize that which we regard with honor.

After an individual has received God's love by accepting Christ as Saviour, most evangelical churches ask for public profession of the conversion. We often use Romans 10:9,10 to illustrate the need for going forward publicly. The congregation witnesses and acknowledges the new believer.

The significant events in our lives should include ceremony. Despite what many young and some older people believe, we do need rituals in our lives. In the musical *Fiddler on the Roof*, Tevya sings to his strong belief in rituals and traditions. Social science research too supports the need for the formation of covenants which are witnessed by others. They help provide us with meaning, transition, recognition, and encouragement to ourselves and others. In addition to being a reminder to ourselves, covenants tell the world that the action we have taken is important.

In America the important relationship of friendship is devoid of any type of ceremony and covenant formation. When men decide to be friends, rarely is there a public commitment, testimony, or acknowledgment by family and friends.

The Bible, however, encourages the establishment of a covenant when men become friends. Jonathan and David, because of their mutual love, decided to make a covenant. A covenant is a promise, a contract, a binding agreement, a formation of unity. "The soul of Jonathan was knit to the soul of David." *Knit*, a term which means "to unite," is the same word used in Genesis to express Jacob's love for his youngest son, Benjamin.

To outwardly show his inward love, Jonathan took off his robe, tunic, sword, bow, and belt and gave them all to his dear friend, David. This symbolic gesture, this outward expression of Jonathan's love, affected greatly their commitment to each other. David, being a peasant and therefore not wealthy, could return only the gift of loyalty and respect to his dear friend.

The giving and accepting of a monetary token which represents commitment helps to solidify friendships similar to the exchanging of rings during a wedding ceremony. Friends can give gifts and remember important days and anniversaries with cards, calls, and letters. These expressions of our friendship should be thoughtful, personal, and creative. I still use the pencil sharpener a friend gave me when I entered college. I still smile when I think of the friend who gave me a sapling for my birthday. He knew I wanted more shade in the backyard of our home.

The gifts are appreciated but it is the giver, the one who thought of me, that I cherish. We need to be more aware of the importance of friends and to take our commitment to them more seriously. In short, we should form covenants with friends. It is vital that friends know that we care about them personally. The very least we should do is to tell them we highly value them and our relationship with them.

Principle #3: Faithfulness

There are few things more irritating than someone who is unpredictable and cannot be counted on when you really need him. In Proverbs 14:20 and 19:4 we read that wealth adds many friends. These fair-weather friends are bad news. These people are plentiful, but not worth very much. The writer of Proverbs says that a true friend "sticks closer than a brother" (18:24) and, "Do not forsake your friend" (27:10).

While the world's philosophy tends to be "Laugh and the world laughs with you, cry and you cry alone," biblical friendship calls for faithfulness. Circumstances should not affect our consistency. In Romans 12:15 Paul tells us to "rejoice with those who rejoice," and to "weep with those who weep" (*RSV*).

I'm reminded of Job's three friends when I read Proverbs 25:19, "Trust in a faithless man in time of trouble is like a bad tooth or a foot that slips" (*RSV*). This is, to say the least, a rather graphic illustration of the grief one suffers from an unfaithful friend.

It seems that unfaithfulness often rears its ugly head at

times when we are most vulnerable. Sickness, unemployment, or poverty can quickly thin the ranks of friends. Last year a popular young woman my wife knows quite well went through a tragic divorce. We were very surprised for this was the "model couple." He fell for the charms of his secretary. Everyone was shocked and his wife was devastated. During and following the divorce she needed the love, companionship, and support of her friends. And yet at this time in her life when she needed reassurance, some of her friends began to give her the cold shoulder. How could this happen?

So much of our social lives are structured in couple-oriented activities, and now that Carol was alone she was no longer part of her old married group. I think the rejection goes deeper, however. Carol was now an unattached attractive woman who was perceived not as a lonely grief-stricken person who needed her friends during a difficult period but rather as a threat. *Who knows? Maybe she'll try to steal my husband*, must have been the conscious or unconscious reasoning on the part of the women who abandoned her in her time of need. The insecurities of these women prevented them from being faithful to a friend.

Faithfulness is critical to a close relationship because we trust and depend upon those who are close to us. Christ's deepest hurts occurred within His circle of closest companions in whom He trusted. David was wounded emotionally more by the treachery of his close friends than by the efforts of his enemies. He laments in Psalm 55:12-14, "If an enemy were insulting me, I could endure it; if a foe were raising himself against me, I could hide from him. But it is you, a man like myself, my companion, my close friend, with whom I once enjoyed sweet fellowship as we walked with the throng at the house of God." Paul too was left to stand alone when he was deserted by Demas and others.

A faithful friend keeps confidences. Again in Proverbs (16:28) we read that "a perverse man stirs up dissension and a gossip separates close friends." And in 17:9, "He who covers over an offense promotes love, but whoever repeats the matter separates close friends."

There is a vulnerability in friendship, and this is as it should be. This is one reason why betrayal is so evil and faithfulness so virtuous.

Principle #4: Social Involvement

In our highly mobile society where approximately 20 percent of our population moves annually, few men are willing to form lasting commitments to a community or to individuals. And yet the Scripture admonishes us to be good neighbors, involved in the lives of others. Neighbors are a form of friendship.

A good neighbor or friend is not only reluctant to start trouble (Prov. 3:29) but is also unwilling to spread it (Prov. 25:8,9). Silence is better than criticism. When I was a boy of 10 or 11 my father told me, "If you can't say something good about somebody don't say anything at all." So often when we spread unflattering or even untruthful statements, we really tell others more about our own character than we do of the person we are condemning. In fact, the Bible says in James 1:26 that the man that "does not keep a tight rein on his tongue,. . . deceives himself and his religion is worthless."

"He who despises his neighbor sins, but blessed is he who is kind to the needy" (Prov. 14:21). When Christ was asked by a lawyer, "Who is my neighbor?" the Lord responded with the parable of the good Samaritan. A man had just left Jerusalem on a trip to Jericho when he was robbed and beaten. The thieves left him to die. A priest and then later a Levite traveled past the victim but refused to get involved. Lacking in the simplest of human compassion these two leaders went on by, leaving the men to die. The next man on the scene was a Samaritan. The Samaritans were social outcasts of Jesus' day, similar to the untouchables of India. This man, the Samaritan, cared for the victim's wounds and took him to a local boarding house to recuperate. He paid an innkeeper for the night and promised to pay for all expenses until the man was well enough to travel.

The principle requires that we get involved in the lives of others. Referring to the Samaritan, Jesus said, "Go and do likewise" (Luke 10:29-37). The lessons from Jesus and the Proverbs should not leave the impression that we must attempt involvement with anyone and everyone. This involvement the Lord calls for is not sentimental. We are to keep our distance from some. Involvement is not unconditional, for the Bible says, "Do not make friends with a hot-tempered man, do not associate with one easily angered" (Prov. 22:24). The psalmist also warns that we not fellowship with the wicked.

A word of caution is needed. We must not avoid people who act or think differently from us and defend our lack of social and spiritual involvement by appealing to the wicked-neighbor argument. Most people we meet will respond favorably to kindness and cordiality if we take the time and trouble to enter into their lives. In the mid 1960s in a suburban Chicago church, I was working with boys in a youth group. One evening while making home visits I met a man who was angry that I had interrupted his favorite TV show. What followed were a few anxious moments, but when he realized that I was concerned about his son he changed his view of me markedly. The conversation improved. A few weeks later he began attending our church on a regular basis. Despite our differences—and they were many—we were able to get along because we at first found an area of common interest, his son.

Along with their wives, married men should take a responsible part in social relationships. Too often men do very little to make or maintain social contact with others. Usually the entire enterprise is left to the wife. It is the wife who schedules social engagements and handles details about children and other family concerns. And if a family moves away, the wife rather than the husband writes letters and sends gifts to maintain the relationship.

I well remember an exception to this generalization. Several years ago following a family move we began the sometimes pleasant (other times unpleasant) task of hunting for a church. In one church a man introduced himself to me and we had a good talk. Why was it good? I suppose because he took a personal interest in me. Without being nosey he was genuinely interested in me as a person. A couple of Sundays later Paul asked my wife and me to join his family for lunch following the worship hour. A couple of weeks later he asked if I would like to help him with the leading of a large Sunday School discussion group on the book of Mark. We worked on the lessons while having an early breakfast together once or twice a month. I'm sure our family would have joined this particular church even if this special friend had not taken an interest in me. But I'm glad he did.

Three years ago I was asked to accept the church nominating committee's recommendation that I serve as chairman of the church. I told the committee that I would need time to think, study, and pray about this request. In my prayers I expressed the gut feeling that I was unqualified for the position. This feeling seemed to be reinforced as I studied the third chapter of 1 Timothy, chapter 1 of Titus and other related Scriptures.

I sought the counsel of my friend Paul. He helped me

to see that my respect for the chairmanship role, along with my feelings of unworthiness, were actually traits that a church leader should possess. He told me I should seek the Lord's guidance rather than depend exclusively upon my own strength. Partially due to this man's support and confidence I accepted the chairmanship.

It's important for us to reach out to others by the investment of our time and concern. We have a responsibility to involve ourselves with other men.

Principle #5: Candor

"Faithful are the wounds of a friend" (Prov. 27:6). "A rebuke impresses a man of discernment" (17:10). Give it to me straight. What do you really think? The friend who will level with you or even rebuke you is far better than one who is insincere, or speaks false words of affection. The biting words of a true friend may hurt your pride and feelings at the moment, but over the long haul you'll be much better off for having heard them. By contrast the flattery or neglect of a false friend can bring you harm in the long run (see Prov. 29:5). Refusing to speak rebuke can also bring harm. David neglected his duty to his son Adonijah and it ultimately cost that son his life (1 Kings 1:6).

A friend will help you face the truth even if you're not too excited at the moment to hear it. The candor of a friend can provide the perspective or point of view needed to help you make wise decisions.

I believe the majority of people feel that arguments are destructive to a relationship and, therefore, differences of opinion should be kept to oneself. This is not necessarily true. Expressing differences does not mean that we do not respect the feelings of others. Actually it's those people who are only our acquaintances that we keep our feelings from, not our close friends. This is also true of differences of opinion. "As iron sharpens iron, so one man sharpens another" (Prov. 27:17). We learn and grow when we listen to different ideas.

A close friend, seeing a need, a personality flaw, or a problem will not remain quiet, even when to do so appears to be the prudent approach. When Moses was having difficulty in his efforts to create a legal social order for the nation of Israel, his father-in-law, Jethro, said, "Listen now to me and I will give you some advice" (Exod. 18:19). Moses was exhausted trying to settle every dispute the people could manufacture. Jethro told Moses his work load was too heavy and suggested he teach others to be fair judges and distribute the judicial load, speeding up the resolution of disputes.

It would have been easier for Jethro to stay out of it. Why take the risk of being ridiculed or accused of meddling or be embarrassed if Moses refused the advice? But Jethro cared for Moses and the nation of Israel and was therefore willing to be candid, and Moses listened and did as his father-in-law suggested.

The willingness to express your own needs is another aspect of this principle of candor. Paul the apostle, after leading a slave to the Lord, sent him back to his master Philemon of Colossae. The slave Onesimus carried a letter from Paul in which he told Philemon to welcome this slave as he would welcome Paul (Philem. 17). Calling for a new relationship, Paul asked Philemon to receive Onesimus as a brother and reminded him in the short letter that Philemon was indebted to him and Paul wanted him to do this favor.

In Matthew 16 Jesus asked the disciples what the people were saying about Him. He then gave them a rather candid question: "Who do you say I am?" (v. 15). Perhaps there was a long silence. Then the impulsive but devoted Peter replied, "You are the Christ, the Son of the living God" (v. 16). There was no doubt about how Peter felt about Jesus, even though there were times when he was a hindrance to Christ.

Possibly the most candid statement in Scripture is Christ's response to Nicodemus in the third chapter of the Gospel of John. The Lord cuts right through to the heart of Nicodemus's problem when He said, "I say to you, unless one is born anew, he cannot see the kingdom of God" (v. 3, *RSV*). Most of the conversations the Lord had with people were very straightforward.

Honest, forthright speech is encouraged by New Testament phrases such as, "speak the truth in love," "Let your yes be yes and your no, no" and "be angry and sin not." But it must be remembered that candor should only be provoked by our love and concern for another's well-being. Also candor is reciprocal; we must be willing to *listen* to our friends' advice to us, not just give it to them.

Candor then, in the biblical sense, means you always have the interests and well-being of the other person in mind when you speak.

Principle #6: Respect

The Bible teaches that each individual is a unique creation of Almighty God. Each of us has inherent worth and dignity, not because of what we can do or produce but, simply and yet profoundly, because we were consciously and purposefully created by the hand of God. Therefore, we should respect the humanness of each person, realizing that God loves each and every individual.

The dictionary defines the verb *respect* as follows: "to feel or show esteem for, to honor, to show consideration for, avoid violation of, treat with deference." Many people feel that close friends having achieved intimacy no longer need to show respect or deference to each other.

These people make a major mistake that the Bible warns against.

The book of Proverbs is rich in teachings on the importance of being tactful and respectful of close friends. Some people trade on or force a friendship by, for example, outstaying a welcome. If I fail to show respect for the need of my friend to be alone, or with his family, or simply to be away from me, I will cause great harm to the relationship. There is truth to the adage "familiarity breeds contempt" if we fail to respect the needs of our friends. We read in Proverbs 25:17, "Seldom set foot in your neighbor's house—too much of you, and he will hate you." Powerful words aren't they? One does not show respect when he is thoughtless or takes advantage of an intimate friendship. A friend should be considerate and tactful.

A lack of respect will hinder or destroy the best of relationships. Two men I know are no longer close friends because of this issue of respect. They still speak and on occasion, along with their wives, will spend an evening together. But the great love that existed for years between these two has vanished.

I asked each man what had happened. "Bill is cold and aloof. He refuses to take my advice. And besides, his emphasis on material things has affected his love for God." When I asked Bill about this situation he said that his friend has attempted to invade both his home and his beliefs, violating the principle of mutual respect. "He was unhappy with our middle-class life-style and was vocal about it in subtle ways. Henry will come to my house with his family, spend the entire weekend, eat my food, allow his kids to break the furniture, and finally leave without a word of thanks. The final straw came when he told my wife she was not studying the Bible correctly and should follow his method." Their responses are sad; with more respect and better communication the rift could have been prevented.

We need to be reminded that the closest of friendships need guarding if they are to be maintained. Within our closeness we must respect each other's individuality.

An ingredient in the recipe of respect is toleration of individual differences. To be able to do this you must see things from another's point of view. And you must then give him the time and space and respect to be what even God has allowed him to be.

David knew Jonathan was the king's son. He could have viewed him as the heir to the throne of the man who wanted him dead. On the other hand, Jonathan could have viewed David as an aggressive and rebellious peasant who was trying to destroy his father's reign as king of Israel. Neither of these young men resorted to a limited, narrow view of the other. Rather, they embraced each other as total human beings and therefore allowed each other the right to be individuals.

Christ's Example

The best illustration of friendship is given to us in the life of Jesus Christ. His interaction with others provides us with countless examples that we can hold up as our goal for dealing with other men. I recommend that you read with care the words and deeds of Jesus as recorded in the historical Gospels.

Remember it didn't and still doesn't matter to Christ who you are or what your background is. For He loves unconditionally. In 1 John 4:10, John tells us, "This is love: not that we loved God, but that he loved us and sent his Son as an atoning sacrifice for our sins." John continues with the ultimate challenge, "Dear friends, since God so loved us, we also ought to love one another" (v. 11). Paul also, in Romans 5:6-10, comments on Christ's great love.

Our goal is to love others. Indeed the very mark of the Christian and the command of Christ is that we love one another (John 13:35). Love is at the foundation of each of the biblical principles mentioned in this chapter. Love is at the foundation of all that is meaningful in our relationships with others.

Discussion Questions

1. Discuss several ways on how to begin friendships. Do your answers vary depending on the personality of each potential friend or the context in which you meet?

2. What do you feel are five major obligations you have to each of your friends? What five things should you be able to respect in return?

3. What rituals and/or ceremonies for friendship would you be comfortable with in your personal relationships?

4. What are several dangers in saying, as Jethro did to Moses, "Listen now to me and I will give you some advice"? How can you protect against these same dangers and yet practice candor?

5. How do you resolve the dilemma of both respecting the individuality of your friends and yet wanting what's best for them as you see it?

Chapter 5

Friendship Qualities Men Look for in Others

"The porcupine, whom we must handle gloved, may be respected, but is never loved." *Arthur Guiterman*

Who are the most important people in your life? Who are the people who have influenced you positively? Who do you care about?

I have asked these questions of men for many years. Usually the answers include parents, brothers or sisters, and perhaps a teacher—and sometimes, close friends.

I also ask, Why are these people so important to you? What makes them so different from the hundreds of others you know? What attracts you to them? The answers are strangely similar, centering on six significant personality qualities: acceptance, empathy, willingness to listen, loyalty, self-disclosure, and compromise.

These basic human traits will draw men together. Each of the six requires an element of love. They overlap somewhat, but they are useful to consider as we discuss what men look for in close relationships.

Acceptance

"Bill accepts me just for what I am. He doesn't try to make me into something I'm not."

A retired man told me that he felt accepted and loved by his wife because "she doesn't hold grudges." He added, "She gets mad at me, sure, but she gets over it in a hurry."

Some people never seem to *forget*—an essential quality in forgiving. Sure, everyone gets angry, but we need to deal with it, not let it stew for long periods. The Bible says, "Do not let the sun go down while you are still angry" (Eph. 4:26). The Ephesian letter warns us to "get rid of all bitterness, rage and anger, brawling and slander, along with every form of malice. Be kind and compassionate to one another, forgiving each other, just as in Christ God forgave you" (vv. 31,32). To forgive, to let anger subside, is to accept others as humans, capable of making mistakes.

A successful businessman once told me he wanted a divorce because his wife was no longer "interesting" to him. He had an image of what a perfect wife should be, and since his wife failed to measure up he wanted out. It's no surprise that his wife is a broken woman; she tried hard to measure up, but she failed. He needed to see his wife as she was, not as he hoped she would be.

An intelligent college student said, "I had to face the fact that personalities don't always blend perfectly." We need to get beyond the "I'm right, you're wrong" trap. A better approach is, "We're different; let's accept that." Unity need not mean uniformity. We need to accept one another despite differences.

Dr. Carl Rodgers, the noted psychologist, says that if we want to build relationships, if we want to learn to accept others, we must "destroy the idea of what a per-

son should be." A woman constantly bugged her husband to take out the garbage until he said, "As soon as
you stop nagging, I'll take it out." A woman addicted to
cigarettes complained to Ann Landers about how her
husband nagged her about her habit. "I need his compassion, not his scolding."

Few people change when they're told to, even if it's
"for their own good." When we stop trying to change
people and simply accept them the way they are—even
with their irritating habits—we put people at ease. They
feel loved—and ironically, are more likely to change.

On my informal surveys, people often say of an
accepting friend, "He realizes he's not perfect and I guess
that makes him more willing to accept my imperfections."
If we admit that we have faults we're more likely to be
sympathetic to the imperfections of others. Matthew's
Gospel (7:3) asks, "Why do you look at the speck of saw-
dust in your brother's eye and pay no attention to the
plank in your own eye?"

A boy caught red-handed in mischief by his mother
tearfully asked, "Do you love me anyway?" We never
outgrow the need for assurance that someone truly loves
us. The key to close relationships is "being loved anyway." That's acceptance.

Empathy

"When I have a serious problem my friend asks what
are *we* going to do about it? Can you imagine that I am
so lucky as to have a friend who is willing to share problems as well as joys?" The New Testament says we
should "rejoice with those who rejoice, weep with those
who weep" (Rom. 12:15, RSV).

One man responded on a questionnaire, "Usually I
don't like it when someone responds to my grief with 'I
know how you feel.' They don't know how I feel." This

man was not afraid of a close relationship. He did, however, resent superficiality. We need to get beyond the perfunctory.

I'm convinced that some of the deepest friendships develop during sorrow. If we shrink from others when they are in need, we miss the opportunity to help and we miss the chance to build a friendship.

During the 1980 presidential primary season, *Newsweek* magazine told this story about George Bush: While a boy in school, the future vice-president was with a group of boys who laughed at a fat youngster stuck in a playground tunnel. Rather than join the laughter, George ran to his side and helped push him through, apparently unconcerned about what the gang might think.

A true friend will come to your aid even if it's unpopular, for he's interested in you. When we are concerned with others we tend to be less aware of ourselves. It's ironic how happiness eludes those who seek it directly, often by self-indulgence. But the person who takes on the burden of concern for the welfare of others, discovers, sometimes surprisingly, that he has obtained happiness indirectly.

To identify with, means to treat people as equals. A retired schoolteacher told me she can often tell if someone has a child's heart by his/her body language. The person who cares will kneel and speak to the little person at his or her level—eye to eye.

While a senior in college I did substitute teaching in a third-grade class at Harrison School on the west side of South Bend, Indiana. I learned a valuable lesson. It was the custom of each student, upon entering the room in the morning, to give 25 cents to the teacher to be held and then distributed just before lunch.

The first day I pinch-hit for the regular teacher, one of the boys took a quarter out of the desk before we broke for lunch. At lunchtime I was short one quarter. After I found out who had taken the money, I sent the other children on to lunch. Billy had taken the money because he was hungry. He came from a poverty-stricken and broken home and was often sent to school with neither breakfast nor money for lunch. It would have been easy to chastise him; and it was necessary, of course, to help Billy see that it was wrong to take someone else's quarter.

Still, there sat before me a hungry boy. The school provided him a lunch that day and began work on getting him into their lunch program.

The next day, in came the children with their books and quarters. I talked with Billy during a break and, while he was surprised, he was eager to pass out the quarters just before lunch. He was happy that someone had tried to understand him and his problems. We need to take the time to understand and to trust, to risk ourselves—and maybe a few quarters—to leave a positive impression upon the lives of others. We need more than just talk; we need to enter into people's lives and problems.

Listening

"He's always willing to hear what I have to say. I never have to feel that my small problems are unimportant." One lady responded to my survey, "At the end of a long day of homemaking I need to talk to my husband. You know, he really listens. I love him."

Our culture seems to say that talking is more important than listening. We respect and admire great orators, but who are the great listeners of our society? The question may seem silly, but nevertheless what the world needs is more listeners. Almost everyone I surveyed placed high value on a person who would listen.

We use four basic communication skills: reading, writing, speaking and listening. You can take a course in any one of the first three, but seldom do you ever hear of a course in how to listen. If men would learn to listen to each other, we would put many psychologists and psychiatrists out of work.

A friend told me about a counseling session he had with a woman who was having serious problems with her husband. The problem was so distressing that my friend felt unable to offer any meaningful help. After listening to her for nearly an hour he apologized for being unable to offer a solution. Surprisingly, the lady responded, "You have helped me so much. I feel better now." He had helped her by simply giving her his full attention for a few important minutes.

Some people listen only for a break in the conversation so they can say what's on their mind. Often we even miss the point of what someone is saying because we are so concerned with what we are going to say next.

William Gladstone and Benjamin Disraeli, British statesmen, were famous contemporaries and each served as prime minister during the long reign of Queen Victoria. Asked about her impressions of the two men, the queen said that when she was with Gladstone, "I feel I'm with one of the most important leaders in the world." About Disraeli she said, "He makes me feel as if I am one of the most important people in the world." She admired Gladstone, but admiration does not always lead to intimacy. The queen's comment about Disraeli was likely due to his desire to learn more about her. He was interested in her.

During a convention at Notre Dame University in 1969 I had the opportunity to spend a few minutes alone with former Supreme Court Justice Earl Warren. The meeting is memorable not simply because he was an important public figure, but because he gave me his full attention for those brief minutes. This gentle man listened to my questions completely and then gave me thoughtful answers, resulting in a lasting and good memory of the meeting.

Prevalent in our culture is our failure to "hear" the feelings and needs our acquaintances have when they speak to us. And if they perceive that we are not truly hearing—at the feeling level—they will, of course, stop sharing.

Even our body language can tell others if we are listening or not. Looking around the room or at your watch instead of at the person, communicates a lack of interest. Sadly some men actually plan to be detached and unavailable. We need to be aware of our gestures and behavior.

It has been my professional responsibility to teach students and to be sensitive to their needs. Sometimes following a long day, I'd come home planning to relax. If I was not careful—and sometimes I wasn't—I'd not listen well to my wife and children who needed my attention. I needed their attention too, and the best way to get attention is to be willing to give it.

Genuinely listening is an act of recognition. In a sense you're saying, "You are important to me; I care about you and what you say," an important ingredient in friendship building.

Loyalty

"When I tell Howard something in confidence I know he will not spread it around town."

"He means what he says."

"If my close friend thinks I'm doing something self-destructive, he'll tell me."

The loyal friend will not be two-faced. Gossip is cancerous to friendships. Immature people tend to gossip to gain attention. A loyal friend avoids these destructive conversations. A loyal friend will be honest with you, even if he thinks you want to hear something else. A loyal friend knows that insincerity, even expressed as praise, is likely to hinder a relationship.

In my study I have a picture of dozens of beautiful old redwood trees. The caption reads, "Quality endures." Quality relationships endure the test of time mainly because of the loyalty of friends.

People who responded to my questionnaire valued friends who do what they say they will do, who can be counted on to follow through with commitments. The loyal friend honors long-range commitments, not easy in our fast-paced culture.

In his best-seller *Future Shock* Alvin Toffler says that ours is a throwaway society where even friendships are temporary. Commitments to friends, job, community, country and even family appear to be on the decline. The resulting lack of intimacy contributes to countless personal and social problems. Juvenile delinquency, divorce, mental illness and child abuse are only a few examples.

The tragic irony is that many, in an effort to purge themselves of the unhappiness and loneliness caused by a lack of committed friends, actually want even more independence. We live in the so-called "me generation" where smart people "look out for number one." Some take assertiveness training, others demand their own rights. While this what's-in-it-for-me trend can help people with low self-images, overall it's destructive. If we neglect the needs of others, we all suffer.

In his book *The Friendship Factor*, Alan Loy McGinnis describes a husband who had recently lost both his job and his self-confidence. He had little money. He became difficult to live with. He became impotent. His loyal wife, believing in her lifelong commitment to her husband, knew he needed her now more than ever. McGinnis says there are periods in any relationship when one does most of the giving. This is a test of loyalty.

A close friend of mine has two aging parents, both of whom require help each day just to carry on with simple tasks. Helping his folks in their time of need is evidence of his commitment.

My wife has a friend from her high school days who was both pretty and intelligent. She went on to college and graduate school and eventually received a master's degree in chemistry. Soon after she began her teaching career she married a wonderful, handsome guy. One evening some eight years later she complained of a severe headache.

Unfortunately the emergency room physician did not feel her condition was serious. It was not until the next day that it was discovered that she had contracted spinal meningitis. It's been nearly ten years since Jerry learned that his wife would never be her normal self. She has difficulty reasoning or doing simple tasks. In many ways her behavior is childish. Jerry's dream of intellectual companionship and of a normal family life will never come true.

Despite this, he and his wife are still together and appear happy. He is not grudgingly meeting this responsibility—although there are bad days—but rather he made a commitment to the woman he loves, and he is living out that commitment.

Most of us will not be called upon to show our loyalty to a friend or mate by having to make great sacrifices. Regardless of our situation we need to look beyond our own needs. We need to stick by our friends. This may seem strange to the what's-in-it-for-me crowd, but with the help of God, this is how one gives and receives happiness.

Self-Disclosure

"John called on me when he needed help; I didn't feel imposed upon; in fact, I felt privileged he turned to me."

"Becky lets me know what her own needs are."

"Marty doesn't try to pretend she doesn't have problems too."

"I feel a part of his life."

On every questionnaire, respondents said that those closest to them are people willing to disclose their feelings and needs. We often fail to open ourselves to others out of fear of rejection. If you open up, you take a risk. You become vulnerable.

Since dependency is often interpreted as weakness, men tend to fear sharing their emotions with others.

Of course, you shouldn't disclose your needs to those who are not interested. But as a relationship develops it is only natural that individuals share needs, problems, expectations, fears, wants, and even weaknesses. If you hide or present an unreal front, you may be viewed as unapproachable. Then friendships remain superficial.

Don't be afraid to ask for help. No one wants to be a pest, but too often the I-don't-want-to-be-a-burden argument is a smokescreen protecting us from a closer relationship.

Strange as it may seem at first, people feel warm toward those who are willing to receive. We hear it is more blessed to give than to receive. While this injunction is true, it doesn't mean we shouldn't receive. Too many are stingy receivers. Jesus often began a new relationship by asking for food, lodging or fellowship. We often withdraw from people who seem to be self-sufficient. With His willingness to receive, Christ gave others an opportunity to give. We like to help. We want to be useful. Talk to virtually any elderly American and he will tell you that he wants to be useful. We do no one a favor by removing opportunities for them to contribute to the lives of others.

A friend I liked a great deal was older than I and had accumulated a good deal of wisdom. He was willing to share with me, and I was grateful for his positive influence. After a time, however, I felt somewhat uneasy. I think I now know what the problem was. I was always on the receiving end of the friendship. My friend conveyed the impression that he didn't have any needs. He was a kind man and willing to give of himself, but he was unwilling to ask others for help.

When a person feels needed, he feels important. A school administrator could not understand why the teachers in his district were grumbling and generally suffering from low morale. After all, why should they complain? They were among the best-paid faculty in all of Wisconsin. But they did not feel needed or important. Since collective bargaining was introduced in the school system, an adversary relationship was established. Teachers, while well paid, were no longer recognized for a job well done.

We never outgrow our need to be a necessary member of some group. We need to feel important. We need to be told we're doing a good job. Many psychologists feel that a major reason retirement is such a difficult adjustment for most men is that they no longer have the sense of being needed.

In addition to the fear of rejection, we tend to hold people off at arm's length because we want to be admired. If people knew our true selves, without our social masks, they wouldn't admire us—or so our reasoning goes. It's unfortunate that we are not more transparent. The emotionally secure individual expects to like and trust others. He also expects to be liked by others, and is therefore less likely to feel a need to hide.

Openness produces openness. Proverbs advises that to have friends, we need to be friendly. Friendships must be reciprocal.

Compromise

"I'm glad Bob doesn't always insist on getting his own way."

"Bill is willing to consider what I think."

Some men think being firm and unaltering in their decisions is a sign of strength. But how can it be weakness to be sensitive to others?

Psychologist Clyde Narramore believes that one sign of the mentally healthy person is being neither a dictator nor a doormat. Narramore encourages us to both have and express convictions, but not to the extent that we disregard the convictions and feelings of others.

An unwillingness to compromise is actually a manifestation of immaturity. A young woman said, "When I was dating, I liked being told what to do. Now I've grown up and I don't like men who are rigid and insensitive to my ideas."

Friends compromise on matters of personal convenience not on matters of personal values or principles. The dictionary defines *compromise* as "a settlement of differences in which each side makes concessions." A suburban housewife said that if her husband, just once in a while, was willing to take her to a concert or out to dinner she wouldn't mind spending two weeks each summer with him on a fishing trip to northern Wisconsin. If we compromise, others compromise, allowing friendships to develop.

These six qualities of friendship we look for in others are important if we truly want to develop intimate emotional relationships. Now for the hard question: Do you have these traits that you look for in others?

Discussion Questions

1. Which qualities of friendship listed in this chapter do you and the important people in your life possess?

2. Discuss the meaning of this statement: "Friends compromise on matters of personal convenience, not on matters of personal principles."

3. In what ways is listening an important communication skill in the making and keeping of friendships?

4. Having read chapters 4 and 5 you are probably aware of the indirect relationships between biblical principles and positive friendship qualities. They do not compare completely, but there is a relationship between biblical principles and positive influential personality traits. Use the following chart for discussion.

Friendship qualities we look for in others	*Biblical principles of friendship*
empathy	God-centered
acceptance	covenant formation
listening	respect
loyalty	faithfulness
self-disclosure	candor
compromise	involvement

Chapter 6
The Stages of Friendship

"Be slow to fall into friendship; but when thou art in, continue firm and constant." *Socrates*

We are admonished to love everyone, but must we love all individuals with the same intensity and involvement? Of course you can't do it, but should your love be somehow divided equally among the people you know? And should you feel guilt because you have failed to live up to those democratic expectations? Each of these questions deserves a definite answer of no. Scripture requires that we love others, to be sure, but this love is bound to take different forms and be expressed in many different ways. Biblical principles of love and friendship are just that, principles. Like all principles they should be applied differently, depending on how well you know and how deeply you care for another man.

Jesus formed friendships easily with men and women as well as with children. People with different social positions and views of the world were drawn to Him. Many were aware of His love and concern for them as individuals. But despite His agape love for each and every person, He related to people differently.

It's a basic truth but many are surprised to learn that the Lord did not treat everyone the same. From His large group of followers and disciples, Christ felt the need to select a small group of 12 men to work and fellowship with more intimately. This important and assumingly difficult selection process was preceded by a night of prayer.

Who were the men Jesus picked to work closely with Him? The apostles were an earthly, diverse group of humanity. They were not the men we have stereotyped and immortalized in stained glass. The almost effeminate and saintly mental images many harbor do not represent the men who were closest to the Saviour. Their personalities contained flaws as well as virtues. Most were very young fishermen who labored with their hands. They had little education and no training in theology. Only three left a written account; the remaining nine were probably illiterate. In the entire group, there was not a priest or a single member of the upper class. These, then, were ordinary, common men who usually failed to understand His teachings and occasionally even undermined His efforts because of personal ambitions.

Jesus developed friendships with non-perfect people, providing us an important example. We're rather foolish and ethnocentric if we expect perfection from our friends. Jesus selected imperfect men not just to advance the kingdom of God but because, in His humanness, He too needed fellowship. The large crowds that followed Him around Galilee could not satisfy the need for close friendship.

Christ developed closer relationships with the apostles than He did with other devoted followers. And within the group of 12 were three who shared even greater companionship with Him. Jesus developed a more advanced stage of friendship with Peter, James and John than He did with the others. Even among the three, Jesus was closer to the Apostle John than to Peter or James.

The biographical account of Christ's life provides evidence that it is not only undesirable, it's impossible to treat everyone in the same fashion. Experts estimate that each of us has a pool of from 500 to 2,500 acquaintances. Each of us confides and feels closer to some individuals than to others. This is quite natural since we don't have either the emotional capacity or the time to share intimately with everyone. And not everyone we know has the emotional energy, time, or desire to be very close to us. If we are sensitive to this latter fact it will help us overcome feelings of being neglected by other men.

Some men develop close friends rapidly. Jonathan and David are one example. Others develop closeness over a longer period of time, like Peter and Paul. And still others, like Job and Eliphaz, never manage to strike up a true friendship. While the time required to cultivate a friendship may vary, all friendships go through specific stages. And in each stage our words, thoughts, and actions are different. Where we are in a relationship affects how we behave.

There are at least three distinct stages or levels of interpersonal relationships. For convenience we will refer to these levels as acquaintance, companionship, and established friendship. This chapter will examine each stage and will also suggest ways to maintain a close friendship.

Acquaintance

An acquaintance can be a stranger at a party, an interesting person we meet on an airplane and know only for a few short hours, or a next-door neighbor we may have known for several years. Length of time we know an individual is not important in an acquaintance relationship. Many of us have worked for years with individuals we do not know well or feel close to emotionally. These people are and probably will remain mere acquaintances.

Conversation with acquaintances is sporadic and rarely goes beyond "safe topics." These could include shop talk, the best fertilizer to use on the lawn, the weather or one's golf game. Safe topics have low emotional content and allow us the freedom to talk while, at the same time, we keep under wraps our beliefs, feelings, fears, hopes, weaknesses, and strengths. The subjects which contain high emotional content are inappropriate conversation topics at this level.

A relationship that is at the acquaintance stage is likely to be based upon where we live or work rather than upon common values or even common goals. If we move, change jobs, or shop in a different part of town, we drop our casual acquaintance relationships in the old neighborhood, at our previous jobs or at the local stores. Most of these relationships form because of what sociologists refer to as *propinquity* or physical nearness and are devoid of emotional commitment. The relationships are for convenience only and will quickly disintegrate if we remove ourselves from day-to-day contact with the people. No real reason exists to maintain the relationship.

In many circumstances it is advantageous to maintain impersonal relationships. For example, business, legal, educational and military interpersonal contacts are formalized and impersonal. Max Weber, the nineteenth-century German sociologist, in his classic studies of bureaucracy, recognized the wisdom of formalizing certain kinds of human interaction in order to maintain objectivity, impartiality, and equality of treatment. Theoretically, favoritism is not an issue in bureaucratic decision making.

Who shall be promoted may be decided on the basis of ability rather than friendship or nepotism.

But impersonality within corporate America is often carried to extremes. Men who are merely acquaintances can at least look at each other and exchange a brief pleasantry on occasion. Men need to shed the stern face and learn to smile more often.

In the early years of the Carter presidency, the press satirized his large teeth which he revealed when he smiled. With the pressures of the job, along with media criticism, the president stopped smiling. But we can learn from his example. President Reagan has a disarming charm that is also a refreshing change in official Washington. One need not be a close companion to extend courtesies to those we come in contact with during a normal day.

People become more pleasant as we get to know them. We miss much by not getting to know each other well enough to get beyond the facade or front that all men don to meet the world.

A friend of mine, Dr. Jay Thompson of Ball State University, is working with foremen in factories for the purpose of improving communication between workmen at different levels of responsibility. The foremen are encouraged to apply simple psychological principles in working with the men and women on the assembly line. Such common niceties as greeting workers with a "hello" or "how's it going" is truly appreciated. The foremen also are encouraged to praise good workmanship and to use positive rather than negative reinforcement. In short Dr. Thompson encourages these men and women to "be nice" to the people they work with. The result is a more pleasant working relationship for everyone.

There is a footnote to this story. One of the foremen told Dr. Thompson, "Ya know, my wife and I are getting along better lately." Courtesy, kindness, and thoughtfulness are principles that apply to all human relationships, regardless of the depth of personal commitment.

Put people at ease in your presence. The writer of Hebrews tells us to "show hospitality to strangers" (Heb. 13:2, *RSV*). The very least we should do at this stage is to make a specific conscious effort to learn the name of and something about our new acquaintance. Be pleasant; ask questions that reveal both interest and acceptance; listen well to what he says; when you meet a second time, use his name—he'll appreciate the fact that you thought enough of him to at least remember his name. Also, ask a question or make some comment about your earlier conversation.

The key to an enjoyable, long-standing acquaintance relationship, such as with a fellow employee at work, is to be pleasant and simply treat the other person in the fashion you would expect to be treated—the "Golden Rule" approach.

Herb Goldberg, in his widely read book *The Hazards of Being Male*, argues that it is extremely difficult for a man to progress beyond the first and superficial stage of interpersonal relationships. Goldberg attributes this inability to early negative conditioning. "By college days all men have already been thoroughly contaminated by the competitive posture which undermines the possibility of genuine intimacy."[11] Male relationships therefore, according to Goldberg, begin and remain at a manipulative level.

Following 10 years of research, Daniel Levinson, commenting about the topic of male friendship, said, "In our interviews, friendship was largely noticeable by its absence. Close friendship with a man or a woman is rarely experienced by American men."[12] These are strong and pessimistic words expressed by both Goldberg and

Levinson; however, other social scientists also feel that male relationships, if they exist at all, are usually superficial and self-serving.

Bensman and Zilienfeld conclude from their research that young individuals "work to create friendships outside the family in an effort to create a self independent of the family, and to develop defenses against family invasions of an autonomous self."[13] Here we have additional negative comment. But while many men form relationships that remain at a shallow level, those who understand and apply biblical principles of friendship can develop deeper, more meaningful relationships.

An acquaintance relationship, while lacking in emotional attachment, need not be self-serving or manipulative, as the researchers would suggest. On the other hand, relationships must remain shallow if the parties are only interested in what's in it for them. Men may progress to higher levels of relationship if they are cognizant of and apply biblical principles of friendship. A proverb says that "a few close friends are more valuable than a host of acquaintances." This is true, but it's also true that all close friendships were at one time mere acquaintances. Don't underestimate your opportunity to formulate companions or friends from people you know who are now only acquaintances. But don't wait. Get started today.

Author Tom Powers says, "We speak, when we speak at all, of neutral things and take a long time to be at ease with each other, and let years go by just as if we had five lifetimes in which to be friends and could afford to squander this one."[14]

Companionship

If acquaintances hit it off and are able to communicate and share something in common, they form what may be termed a *companionship*. Sharing something in common is a vital ingredient to a companionship. At this stage men share common goals rather than common core values. Men join teams, flirt with girls, and go off to war together. Their togetherness is often based on a task to be performed or a goal to be obtained. Goldberg says that men can come comfortably close to each other only when they are sharing a common target. While *target* is a word too narrow and too negative in connotation, it nevertheless is often appropriate.

Researchers Shils and Janowitz, in 1948, conducted a study of the cohesion and disintegration of the Nazi army. Although outnumbered and while being beaten badly, the German soldiers fought on with great effectiveness. Many believed their tenacity was attributed to their strong political convictions. The study revealed, however, that the commitment to fight was related to membership in a squad. As long as the small group members both gave and received affection from each other they were prepared to fight regardless of their individual political attitudes. Buddyships or companionships are formed and sustained because of common goals or a feeling of belonging rather than from common values.

American men are certainly activity and group oriented. We're big on joining groups. Men invented the voluntary association with the first expression probably being freemasonry. Recent examples of popular voluntary male associations are fraternal organizations, country clubs, weekly poker parties, bohemian groups and youth gangs.

Unlike acquaintances, companions schedule time together. There is an effort to go beyond the "Hi, how are you" syndrome that's more of a social custom than a genuine expression of concern. Buddies enjoy each other's company, and although the relationship may exist for many years, usually it is based largely on the immediate satisfactions that come with companionship.

Two lawyers I know have played golf together on a regular basis for many years. They enjoy the togetherness of playing a game but while on the links they make few comments and ask few questions that are not related to the game of golf. They truly do not know each other, but are able nevertheless to enjoy the satisfaction that comes from companionship. Unlike women, men are more able—or perhaps I should say more willing—to departmentalize their lives. I mean by this that men are more willing to relate only to segments or aspects of another's personality. Women, in contrast, assume a holistic approach to human personality.

This companionship level of relationship, while satisfying and even flamboyant at times when things are going well, will not stand up well to emotional stress or individual conflicts of either values or interests. There is little commitment in a companionship, as each man knows that if a real problem occurs he cannot or will not turn to companions for assistance. Men do not seek out a buddy when they need help in time of a personal crisis. This is especially true for men of marginal economic status, as William Whyte and Elliot Liebow have researched and eloquently written about in *Street Corner Society* and *Talley's Corner*, respectively.

Recently, one of the golfing attorneys was quite ill and required emergency surgery. For several days he was in rather serious condition. At their first golf outing the companion said to the fully recovered man, "I hear you were quite ill. Is everything OK now?" The fortunate man responded, "I'm just fine. In fact I'm so good, I'll beat the pants off you out on the course today."

They both laughed and that was it. Nothing else was said about the illness. It's strange somehow, that the man when sick had made no effort to communicate with his companion. And the companion, when hearing of the illness from the clubhouse grapevine, made no effort to contact his buddy. But with the interruption behind them, both were willing to return to their regular weekly round of golf.

Despite the lack of a long-range commitment, companionships serve the important functions of providing fellowship. They give the warm feeling of belonging, similar to the three-Musketeers concept, all for one and one for all.

When we were teenagers we belonged to a peer group that provided us with the good feeling of belonging. Our peers gave us an identity so important to an impressionable teenager. Our group was "in" or "cool" while others were "out" or "out of it," or so we thought. Teens today often categorize themselves and others as freaks, jocks, burnouts (I guess burnouts are the hoodlums of my day) and straights. In your community the names may be slightly different, but these are quite common. But whatever the name attached to a teen peer group, they, like each of us regardless of age, need to establish companionships.

When asked why he returned to coaching football, Bud Wilkinson said, "The emotional aspects of the game are stronger than anywhere else. The feelings you had toward shipmates in World War II, those are the feelings you have in athletics." Companions give a man a feeling of confidence about his value as a man. They are relaxing and yet can provide excitement and diversion from so-called normal activities.

The two most serious problems in achieving and maintaining a buddyship or companionship is trust and dominance, according to Goldberg's research. He suggests that we as men must talk about and understand the kinds of behavior that could destroy confidence we have in each other. Also to handle the issue of dominance, men should consciously work toward equalizing power and decision-making so that neither ends up in the shadow of the other. To accomplish this goal men might arrange tagalong sessions at work or recreation where each man is able to display his strengths and interests.

Companionship may not be friendship, but it is a type of relationship we need. You can deepen a relationship by making an effort to learn more about the men you know as companions. It isn't inappropriate probing to ask questions that are thoughtful and other-person centered. Be trustworthy and dependable, but don't try to appear perfect or all-powerful. If he wants to share a problem, listen well. Companionships need nourishment, for they, like other levels of interpersonal relationships, can be fragile and sensitive emotionally.

Men have frail egos and rarely work at a friendship. We turn off with the slightest provocation or perceived provocation. We hide our true selves from others. Few acquaintances or companionships therefore evolve into actual friendships. While true friendships may be a rarity, they can be obtained if we are willing to invest the necessary time and emotional energy.

Established Friendship

Some seek the fulfillment of needs which companionship alone cannot provide. Companions who share basic similar values and who invest the necessary time and attention can establish friendships. And when a close friendship is established, if it is taken for granted or in other ways neglected, it will slip away from you. Only quality relationships endure.

In chapter 4, we surveyed biblical principles of friendship at some length. In this chapter we will consider the maintenance of established friendships.

"I know that the dissolution of a personal friendship is among the most painful occurrences in human life." So wrote President Jefferson to James Monroe. The ancient Roman Seneca said, "To lose a friend is the greatest of evils."

In a *Psychology Today* magazine study, people were asked to indicate what factors led to a friendship's cooling off or ending. Among the most frequently checked reasons, in the most frequently mentioned order, were:

- One of us moved
- I felt that my friend betrayed me
- We discovered that we had very different views on issues that are important to me
- One of us got married
- My friend became involved with (or married) someone I didn't like
- A friend borrowed money from me
- We took a vacation together
- One of us had a child
- One of us became markedly more successful at work
- I got divorced
- My friend got divorced
- One of us became much richer
- I borrowed money from a friend.[15]

These responses, while interesting, do not reveal the underlying factors leading to a dying friendship, but rather, seem to indicate a sudden breaking off of the relationship. C.S. Lewis said that people do not suddenly renounce their faith in God due to some event or newly acquired insight. Rather, over a long period of neglect, the once strong relationship between man and God slowly dies. This, too, I believe describes a friendship between men that is left largely unattended.

Friendships require the continual application of biblical principles with special attention needed in certain areas. The maintenance of a friendship requires that we not lose sight of three underlying factors. You need to:

1. Commit yourself to your friend
2. Resist judgmental attitudes
3. Accept the love of your friend.

It is after you develop a close friendship with its inherent intimacy that these factors become especially important.

Close friends must consciously establish and renew commitment. Commitments are not popular today. They imply inconvenience. We are bombarded with a self-indulgent, hedonistic ethic that is self- rather than other-person-centered. This aspect of our culture can seep in and work to undermine our friendships. Commitment is not popular and may be a burden, but it is essential to the care and feeding of a friendship.

At a shopping center I saw a girl wearing a tee shirt that read, "If it feels good do it." It's difficult for me to understand how a young woman would display such a phrase without embarrassment, even if she was unaware of the suggestive connotation. This phrase illustrates the self-centered philosophy of our age. This value system implies that "I'll do whatever I want to if it pleases me. And if my pleasure gets in your way—too bad for you." This self-centered value system is the antithesis of the commitment needed to sustain friendship.

Commitment develops slowly and must be protected once it is achieved. Maxine Hancock says, "Commitment is not irrational. It would be foolish to trust a foothold you had not properly tested or to marry a person you have not adequately assessed or to trust a message you have not investigated. But commitment requires more than reason. It requires the act of faith. Then the sense of risk fades and hope grows."[16]

Misfortune is often a test of commitment. When friends come to our aid or defense in time of need, the relationship between us grows more secure and satisfying. We tend to reveal our true colors during times of stress. This truth is illustrated in one of Aesop's Fables, "Two Travelers and a Bear":

"Two Men were traveling in company through a forest, when, all at once, a huge Bear crashed out of the brush near them.

"One of the Men, thinking of his own safety, climbed a tree.

"The other, unable to fight the savage beast alone, threw himself on the ground and lay still, as if he were dead. He had heard that a Bear will not touch a dead body.

"It must have been true for the Bear snuffed at the Man's head awhile, and then, seeming to be satisfied that he was dead, walked away.

"The Man in the tree climbed down.

" 'It looked as if that Bear whispered something in your ear,' he said. 'What did he tell you?'

" 'He said,' answered the other, 'that it was not at all wise to keep company with a fellow who would desert his friend in a moment of danger.' "

The syndicated columnist Sydney Harris said in a recent article that women retain more friends than men because, while men who are friends share activities, women who are friends exchange confidences. I agree, but I can also remember painfully a friend who shared with me in confidence. I reacted too strongly to the problem he shared with me and nearly lost a friend. I was involved in his life and was concerned about his well-being. Knowing this he took a risk and became vulnerable.

The problem was infidelity. When he approached me

he no longer was engaged in the adulterous relationship. He was then trying to contend with and work through his feelings of guilt. He had asked God to forgive his sin but somehow the memory just wouldn't go away. He opened up to me, wanting counsel and acceptance. Unfortunately, I did not follow the Bible's directive for this type of situation. "Brothers, if someone is caught in a sin, you who are spiritual should restore him gently" (Gal. 6:1). Gentle? Not me. Supercilious is a more accurate description of my behavior.

I hardly heard a word he said. It never entered my mind that it must have been difficult for him to share this sin with me. I was too busy moralizing to see his pain. I exerted little effort to understand how he got himself into this predicament. I reacted when I should have acted. Being judgmental I responded emotionally instead of reasonably. I failed. For me to have listened and shown an honest Christian love would not have minimized the sin, but it may have helped a friend who had asked for help.

Despite my insensitivity this friend has maintained our friendship and through the years I've managed to repair the damage I caused. His marriage is back on track, although there are lasting scars.

Quality relationships take time to develop and attention to maintain. You usually can't develop them the moment you are in dire need of a friend. You need to be forming friendships with many people all through life. Your goal in making friends is not simply to have them on hand if you should get into trouble. Friends are for the sharing of common interests and values and for being available to help one another. As you each unselfishly enrich the other's life, you will then be able to minister to each other when needs arise.

A friend is accepted for himself, not as a means to some end. Close friends have love for each other. In one study a full 92 percent believed that friendship is a form of love. The greatest comment on love in all the Bible, and perhaps in all literature, is recorded in 1 Corinthians 13:4-8. Read this brief section of Scripture, being mindful anew of applying its principles to a friendship.

Close friends provide support during trials as well as during accomplishments. They seek to learn the life goals that each has. Friends even help each other to accomplish life goals. Close friends don't ignore character flaws but offer concern and assistance in the correction of possible personality problems. Friends who are less competitive and less defensive may ask for a candid appraisal of personal deficiencies that may be hindering their own emotional or spiritual growth.

While it seems a paradox, friends also respect each other's individuality and independence. While remaining available, friends do not become careless with the other's need to be alone, either physically or mentally. A close friend knows the real you, and loves you anyway. In these relationships there exists encouragement, concern and loyalty.

In earlier chapters we saw that people, regardless of gender, need emotionally supportive relationships. We all have emotional needs which if unmet leave us unhappy or physically or mentally ill. And yet many of us resist. This may well be our biggest problem—the unwillingness to let other people love us, truly love us. We would rather "tough it out" or "grit our teeth" or "take it like a man." Many men, even those who apply biblical principles, tend to go it alone when they have problems.

Perhaps we have a latent fear of being accused of being too close to another man and therefore suspected of being homosexual. More likely, however, we as men have simply been raised to believe the myth that masculinity and independence are synonymous.

The following illustration from an unknown source dealing with medieval knights and dragons illustrates man's dilemma of having both the desire to be close to others as well as the fear of being close.

Within each man there is a dark castle with a fierce dragon to guard the gate. The castle contains a lonely self, a self most men have suppressed, a self they are afraid to show. Instead they present an armored knight—no one is invited inside the castle. The dragon symbolizes the fears and fantasies of masculinity, the leftover stuff of childhood.

When men take the risk and let down the barriers (or drawbridge in the above illustration) people respond to one another as whole persons and try to communicate with openness and intimacy. Openness brings with it opportunity for a growing relationship, for a wider range of deeply felt experiences. This is the stuff from which friendships are formulated and sustained.

Discussion Questions

1. Human flaws become evident when two men become friends. Discuss whether you accept the limitations of others or expect perfection. Remember that Jesus established friendships with imperfect people.

2. Do you know of other stages of friendship that are not mentioned in this chapter? What are they?

3. Christ had friendships with people of different backgrounds and personalities. Discuss how this may be true for you. Should it be?

4. How do you explain the seemingly contradictory feelings of fear and the desire for closeness?

5. How should you respond when a friend confides in you that he has sinned? Use Galatians 6:1 as you consider this question.

Chapter 7
Friendship in Other Times and Places

"A friend is one to whom one may pour out all the contents of one's heart, chaff and grain together, knowing that the gentlest of hands will take and sift it, keep what is worth keeping, and with a breath of kindness, blow the rest away." *Arabian proverb*

Friendship; is it the same wherever you go? Do people understand friendship to mean something specific or does the word have very different meanings depending on one's culture or one's period in history?

We know that the family as a social institution exists in all societies. This is true even for revolutionary societies that have tried to alter or even eliminate family structure. The family is one of God's creation ordinances and exists today in every culture, in every country.

But what about friendship? The information in this chapter should better enable us to understand our own norms, the way we live and think in America, and help us to see that God's principles can be and often are applied in times and places different from our own.

Friendship is ubiquitous in history and in culture. It is integral to the psychological, social, and spiritual health of individuals and societies as is the family structure. Friendship, like marriage and the family, is a gift to us from the Lord. It is for us to protect, nurture, and enjoy.

We often let nationalistic, social and cultural differences cloud the reality that we are but one human race, created by a loving God. Acts 17:26 reads in part that "from one man he made every nation of men." Our feelings and our needs are universal. We need other people.

Dr. Robert Brain, an anthropologist, studied several tribes that are, on the surface, much different from our Western culture. Yet, every one of these tribes manifested a need to reach out to others, a need to make social contact and to formulate friendships. The similarity of humanity is equally in evidence from a sample reading of authors throughout history—Aristotle, Plato, Cicero, Homer, Montaigne, Pascal and C.S. Lewis. Letters or diaries of average people written generations ago reveal the same feeling and needs that we experience today. In many traditions, of course, feelings about friendship and other topics have not been recorded by writers.

Friendship Across the World

Dr. Cora DuBois and several other social scientists have concluded the following from patient cross-cultural research:

1. Friendship is a universal phenomenon. Not every person has the emotional capacity or the social opportunity to develop a friendship but friendship as a relationship occurs in all societies.

2. Friendship is affected by many factors including marriage, sexuality, kinship system and superordinate-subordinate relationships.

3. Friendships are voluntary in that they are not

imposed by the culture or ascribed at birth.

4. Friendships are reciprocal. The action of giving and taking flows both ways.

5. Friendships are dyadic. The most widely valued type of friendship is between two people, although the interpersonal relationship between members of gangs, teams, or clubs has characteristics associated with friendship.

Friendships are between two people. History records effort after effort to establish communes or utopias wherein exist intimate fellowship. Twenty years ago, in the 1960s, we witnessed a resurgent attempt to establish friendship communities or communes. These are almost always doomed to failure. It is hard enough to sustain a dyadic friendship. To sustain a complex multiple intimate friendship is nearly impossible.

Therefore friendship is a personal relationship. Note: In America, friendship is also private, which is a rare phenomenon. Privacy in a personal relationship indicates that the friendship can be established and maintained independent of the different social groups people belong to. In other words, the relationship is autonomous.

6. Friendships are characterized by confidence, trust, and intimacy. The bonding relationship of friendship is an important characteristic of all human cultures.

Assuredly the behavior associated with friendship varies immensely as one travels from culture to culture. But this fact notwithstanding there remains an underlying similarity of beliefs and values associated with this topic that can be discovered in many areas of the world and at different times in the world's history.

When we look beyond the cultural traits we discover core values about friendship that tend to exist on a cross-cultural basis. *The Encyclopedia of Social Sciences* summarizes basic values of friendships that exist in most cultures. Friendship includes closeness, solidarity, absence of ulterior ends, reciprocity, and a playing down of social distinctions such as age, sex, and social class. Friendship obligations and rights are secondary to other, usually family responsibilities. And yet friendship is intimate, important, and enduring. Friendship is associated by rites of passage or ceremonial entry. Friendship involves the exchanging of gifts and/or economic support.

In most cultures, friendship involves voluntary commitment, intimacy, and spontaneity and is valued by the society as a source for personal growth and security. Perhaps this is why to be friendless often involves personal feelings of shame.

Despite differences in customs, every known culture places important emphasis upon the love and loyalty between friends. Anthropologist Robert Brain says that "affection and loyalty are implicit in all friendships in all societies." Undivided loyalty and altruistic love are valued highly throughout the world.

Cultural Universals

In an important book, *The Proper Study of Mankind*, authors Chase and Brunner have cataloged 33 cultural universals of humankind. A cultural universal is an aspect of human behavior that is demonstrated in every, or almost every, culture on the planet. Think of it. Despite the tremendous apparent outward diversity of behavior among the hundreds, perhaps thousands of different cultures within the world's approximately 170 nations, we have much in common. Following is a sample of these universal culture traits.

1. A form of religion and ethic prevail.
2. There is an established government and laws.
3. There is a permanent family structure; monogamy is the usual form of marriage.

4. The family cares for the aged as well as the young.

5. Divorce is recognized but not approved.

6. Society provides punishment for infringements of its rules.

7. The male is the formal ruler of the family and of society.

8. Free giving is a high virtue.

9. There is a sense of loyalty to the nation or tribe.

10. None of the societies has completed communal ownership of property.

11. Friends are limited to the same sex.

Friendship is highly valued and is one of Chase's universal cultural traits. In most cultures a man feels a sense of shame if he lacks an intimate friendship. Aristotle speaks for most cultures when he says that "no one would choose a friendless existence." But this universal belief in the importance of friendships has a restriction.

Perhaps you're surprised by number 11. There probably exists no greater restriction upon friendships than that it must be limited to individuals of the same sex. Both cross-cultural and historical information show that nearly every culture on earth, both now and in generations past, has not cultivated cross-sex friendships.

There is a common belief that men and women can be lovers but never friends. There is evidence that men attempt to develop cross-sex friendships as a means of sexual exploitation. Sociologist Robert Bell found that in cross-sex friendships, the men were usually older and better educated and usually wanted the relationship to end up in the bedroom. Dr. Bell found a high degree of sexuality either implied or expressed in cross-sex friendships. Sexual teasing or actual intercourse results from these relationships. Bell discovered also that usually these cross-sex relationships are superficial and ritualistic.[17]

In a survey conducted by *Psychology Today*, three-fourths of the respondents believed that cross-sex platonic friendships were complicated due to sexual tensions, the lack of encouragement by society, and the fact that man/woman relationships have less in common than friends of the same sex.

If either member of a cross-sex friendship is married, respondents felt that something must be wrong or missing from that marriage. Why else would they need someone other than their spouse for intimate emotional involvement? A spouse is bound to feel threatened by a close cross-sex friendship, partially due to the potential sex problem.

Letty Cotton in *Growing Up Free*, claims correctly that we give too much attention to sex roles. It is true that in a few cultures where women are highly valued, and daily accessibility of members of the opposite sex exists in different areas of life, and where cross-sex platonic friendship is culturally encouraged, a cross-sex friendship can exist, remain nonsexual, and provide emotional satisfaction. The Bangwa of Africa have strong male-female friendships which are never confused with love affairs. But as already noted the Bangwa culture type is extremely rare. Where cross-sex friendships exist at all they tend to be limited to young, unmarried people. Sociologist Bell has found few references to socially approved close friendships between men and women that had no courtship or sexual implications.

We need not be strictly homo-social but the fact remains that in American society our social lives are based on pair relationships, either as marriage partners or as same-sex friends.

Rather than attempt to seek emotional gratification from women other than one's wife, I'm convinced that men need to place more value upon their emotional ties with men.

It seems, from a review of societies existing prior to our own age, that the lives of men and women came together when it was either time to eat or time to go to bed. Throughout American history the major taboos against cross-sex friendship were based on the belief that women were less capable of friendship than men. For example, philosopher George Santayana wrote that "Friendship with a woman is therefore apt to be more or less than friendship; less, because there is no intellectual parity; more, because (even when the relation remains wholly dispassionate, as in respect to old ladies) there is something mysterious and oracular about a woman's mind which inspires a certain instinctive deference and puts it out of the question to judge what she says by male standards."[18]

Christ did not ignore women. On the contrary, during a time when women suffered extreme discrimination, Jesus treated women with respect and dignity. The Zondervan *Pictorial Bible Dictionary* says that, "Godly women were influential in Jesus' background, i.e., Elizabeth, Mary, Anna, the sinner of Luke 7:36-40, Mary Magdalene, Martha and Mary of Bethany, and the women at the empty tomb. But Christ formulated His most intimate friendships with men, Peter, James and John for example."[19]

Privacy or Community

Americans tend to be lonely. Our culture was founded partially on Christian love of God and love of neighbor. But even with this basis, or in spite of it, we are some of the loneliest people on this earth.

In most societies people do not experience loneliness at least to the nagging, acute and painful degree that Americans do. In other cultures people are rarely alone either physically or emotionally. Relatives, neighbors, and even strangers are a normal part of everyone's life.

Not so in America. Our emphasis on privacy has been deadly to our emotional well-being. In most cultures the image of a private, independent life is deserving of sadness. But in America we tend to envy the freedom that comes with the private life. Bachelors are seen as carefree, but in reality they are often lonely and more likely to die sooner than married men.

Anthropologist Robert Brain says that unlike any other culture, our acute loneliness must be seriously considered in any search for solution to nagging contemporary societal problems. Loneliness, and a lack of commitment to others, are factors in our high suicide, divorce, alcoholism, drug, murder, rape, and abortion rates.

Dr. Brain mentions that even the most reserved people, because of loneliness, now look for companionship through special groups such as Parents Without Partners, in singles' bars, gay bars, bleak cocktail parties, and through computer dating. These groups foster an emotional prostitution. One puts on a plastic smile and is for the moment generous with his affection, but only for the moment.

In the artificial ambiance of forced jollity there exists the pathetic hope that a "meaningful relationship" might evolve. But as long as we ignore God's principles for developing a relationship, it of course never will.

People from other cultural backgrounds find it difficult to understand why we cherish personal freedom to such an extreme degree. To them, personal freedom, if understandable at all, would be viewed as a form of isolation, a feeling of being ostracized. With the songwriter they might agree that "freedom means I've nothing left to lose." To many from other times or places, friendship as a social requirement would be far preferable to our autonomous individualism.

Many Western nations including America have sacrificed emotional intimacy on the false altar of personal freedom. Many American males have never experienced a close male friendship or known what it means to love and care for a male friend. Those who do have friends usually have experienced low levels of trust and personal sharing and generally invest little in these relationships. The very few that have established intimate male friendships have done so with at least a degree of guilt and peer ridicule.

The parable of the rich fool (Luke 12:16-20) has several appropriate applications for us today. The man, for example, was a fool because of his (1) inordinate emphasis upon materialism at the expense of sharing and the developing of intimacy with others; (2) his belief that his belongings were his own and were the measure of self-worth and importance; (3) his preoccupation with storing instead of sharing; and (4) his idea that he can feed his soul with bread. This life-style makes no sense to God and is why the man is called a fool.

The rich fool would feel more at home in mainstream America than in many other cultures that are less materialistic and more caring. The rich fool would feel out of place if he were living with the Zuni Indians of New Mexico where cooperation more than competition is the economic norm. People may argue or compete, but the practice is not encouraged. With the Zuni, and in countless other cultures, the respected people are cooperative, friendly, and generous with time and possessions. The respected people are not concerned with accumulating more goods or property than they can use, and if they do acquire wealth they are expected to share. In contrast with the rich fool of Luke 14, the Zuni have a common storehouse where agricultural surplus is put to be shared by all. Emphasis is devoted to developing relationships, not to competition and the accumulation of wealth.

For American men the term *friend* is lacking in content. It is devoid of emotion and of commitment. We rarely know what someone means when he declares that "he is my friend." The word could be used for someone who seems to be pleasant to be with since our first meeting some 30 minutes earlier.

Unlike several other cultures, the American society is less structured, less formal and more free in its social relationships. This social climate which encourages spontaneity has drawbacks as well as advantages. Our relationships are usually shallow, one-dimensional, unfulfilling, and usually short-lived. We have few assurances that our current friends will remain our friends a few months down the road.

In other cultures, friendship, like marriage or the parenting responsibility, is a binding one. In other areas of the world friendship is elevated to a status equal to marriage and is encompassed with ceremony and ritual. The concept of blood brotherhood, for example, is found in most societies.

It is not imperative for friendship to be established with ritual and sustained by specific societal requirements, but anthropologists including Robert Brain have found that in most cultures of the past and present, love between friends has not been allowed to depend upon the vague bonds of mere emotional sentiment alone. Usually a culture will establish specific expectations for friends to abide by, as with other essential social relationships such as with spouse, parents, and children. Dr. Robert Bell says that in America if a friend dies we ought to attend his funeral, but there is no obligation requiring us to do so. But in West Africa and elsewhere when a man dies, his friend must put on filthy rags and perform socially required rituals.

There exists an almost universal practice of gift exchange in the different cultures. This practice is often socially required. In our Western culture this practice has declined in recent decades and is now largely reserved for family members. Americans still exchange Christmas card greetings and on occasion bring a token gift such as a bottle of wine when visiting the home of a friend or neighbor.

Why do people trade gifts that have only slight economic worth? The exchange of small gifts has symbolic rather than monetary significance. A major anthropological study of gift exchange concluded that presents are given to express, solidify, and formulate closer relationships between individuals and groups.

On the surface, certain ceremonial behaviors may have little social significance, but the underlying social meaning and consequence may be profound. Without the ritual and ceremony, and therefore the respect associated with friendship, we have few socially approved guidelines for developing friends. We are set adrift and must depend soley upon the casual accident of getting to know someone.

Robert Brain reports that today on the continent of Africa, cultural behavior among close friends exists and it is comparable to the David and Jonathan ideal. The Bangwa unashamedly sing their friends' praise. Public demonstration of friendship is common. At festivals they dance and sing. At funerals they express their grief through open weeping and even tear at their clothes over the loss of a close friend. The open display of happiness, grief, and other emotions contrasts the American procedure of the male internalizing his God-given feelings, be they happy or sad. Of course there are cultural traits related to friendship norms throughout the world that would not be appealing or morally acceptable to us because of our upbringing or because it might violate a biblical mandate. But we can learn that there are other ways of expressing friendship.

In the West, intimate friendships have been discouraged in favor of the close relationship between husband and wife. But it need not be an either/or relationship. In several Mediterranean countries friendship is of significant emotional importance, as is the family and kinship system. In some cultures such as the Alcala in Andalusia, an agricultural community, the social fabric is bound together with friendship ties as strong and as important as those of kinship.

In numerous simple societies men must meet specific qualifications in order to become friends, and then adhere to stringent social rules to maintain the friendship. We, on the other hand, are hampered by our lack of societal ground rules on how we should conduct ourselves.

Jesus, in the third chapter of Mark's Gospel, seems to extend—and even redefine—our kinship responsibilities and relationships to draw in and include friendship. During a conversation, a group of people told Him that His mother and siblings were outside waiting for Him. His response was, "Who are my mother and my brothers?" Looking around the room He added, "Here are my mother and my brothers! Whoever does God's will is my brother and sister and mother" (vv. 31-35).

It is a myth which states that marriage alone can satisfy all of an individual's emotional needs. Without friends, wives and husbands must rely totally upon each other for emotional support. Many Christian marriages collapse under the weight of this impossible demand. We should not expect our wives to meet all of our emotional needs.

Frederick Herwaldt, pastor of the Onesquethan Reformed Church in Feura Bush, New York, believes correctly that the church should provide Christians with more than just the "how-to's" of marriage. The church must also encourage other long-term supportive relationships where people can become grandparents, uncles, aunts, brothers, and sisters to one another.

Hospitality

One major way we can reach out to others is by being more hospitable. There is hardly a culture that does not encourage or place importance upon hospitality. The Bible provides us with a model on how to practice hospitality. For example Isaiah 58:7 records the following: "I want you to share your food with the hungry and bring right into your own homes those who are helpless, poor and destitute. Clothe those who are cold and don't hide from relatives who need your help" (*TLB*).

And the words of Jesus spoken to His host one Saturday afternoon, "When you give a banquet, invite the poor, the crippled, the lame, the blind, and you will be blessed" (Luke 14:13,14).

Our hospitality is to extend beyond our family and to include the less fortunate—strangers and friends alike. I would like to know how conservative economist Milton Freidman or liberal economist John K. Galbraith would interpret biblical economic theory as recorded by Moses in Leviticus 23:22. The verse reads, "When you reap the harvest of your land, do not reap to the very edges of your field or gather the gleanings of your harvest. Leave them for the poor and the alien. I am the Lord your God."

Most of us have a negative mental image of how people in other cultures receive strangers—usually symbolized by the ubiquitous cooking pot and hungry cannibals. But reality is much different. Missionaries, travelers, and explorers throughout history as well as today usually report that they are treated with hospitality and respect. Anthropologist Robert Brain concludes from cross-cultural research that cooperation and tolerance of outsiders is more often the rule than the exception. Most cultures recognize a duty to be hospitable to strangers. We should do the same.

Through the years some students of mine and youth group members have found a welcome in our home. Several years ago a student I had in class during my very first year of teaching gave Karen B. Mains' book *Open Heart—Open Home* to my wife. The handwritten note on the inside cover reads:

> With love to Sue,
> I thank God for your open heart! So many times these past seven years your home and love have been a sweet refuge to refresh me for the battle awaiting me back at school. Thanks too for making a home for Dave and for your support and prayers and shared life together. Being with you has convinced me that people are valuable—people are more important than things.
> Keep on abounding in love—1 Thessalonians 4:10-11.
> So glad to be your sister and daughter.
> Margo

Margo is a special person to us. The book she gave us deals from cover to cover with how to practically live the biblical mandates of hospitality found in the Leviticus, Isaiah, and Luke verses quoted above. Karen and David Mains have opened up their home. They have developed the gift of hospitality. We can too. Mrs. Mains provides the reader with dozens of creative yet simple ideas on how to be good stewards of both time and resources, while at the same time reaching out to others with the ministry of hospitality. For example in a chapter on entertaining she says:

> Now when we organize a planned evening of dinner and fellowship, my husband asks guests to contribute to the meal. One brings a salad, one a dessert, one an appetizer. It is not important for me to do everything in order for the occasion to be a success. I have four children to raise, a God to know, words to share, wounds to heal. Because I've put away my pride, lovely things occur. People discover they can be hospitable to me. Yes, we can be friends.[20]

We should be given to hospitality. The author of Hebrews reminds us that we might be entertaining angels unawares (Heb. 13:2). The innkeeper in Bethlehem found a place for Joseph and Mary completely unaware of the historical and eternal significance of the night.

There was but one old man in the city of Gibeah who exhibited the ancient virtue of hospitality. The story is recorded in Judges 19:11-28. He was willing to enter the life of another when he asked with concern, in verse 17, "Where are you going? Where did you come from?" Then in verse 20, "You are welcome at my house."

I know such a person as the old man of Gibeah. Several years ago, following my viewing of the *Roots* TV special of Alex Haley's search for his ancestral home on the west coast of Africa, I decided to conduct my own search for ancestors. My quest was richly rewarded. I discovered that I had a first cousin living in Chicago. We arranged for a meeting. I was at first skittish as Grace has serious and numerous physical handicaps, and in recent years has been forced to live in a low-income area on the north side of the city. Her husband and children have preceded her in death. She has been truly tested. Most of us in her situation would be alone and feeling sorry for ourselves. Not this lady. She exercises the gift of hospitality despite her circumstances.

Grace is wonderful. She truly welcomes people to her apartment and into her life and heart. She has few dollars but she has lots of love. She is rich with friends. She loves our children and now that we have moved to Indianapolis she calls and writes to them on a regular basis. We miss her and love her.

In every culture there is a need for intimate, trusting friendships. We all need individuals with whom we can be open and reveal our deepest feelings. There is something amiss with a culture that ignores, takes for granted, or devalues the human bonds that are so important to our physical, psychological, and spiritual health and happiness.

Our answer is not to attempt to emulate friendship customs from cultures that differ significantly from our own any more than we should begin to wash people's feet as Jesus did for the disciples. Our culture and customs are different. Rather than wash feet we should develop the principle of a servant's heart. And rather than copy friendship practices of other cultures we should learn from them, and then within our own culture search for ways to practice biblical principles of friendship on a daily basis.

Discussion Questions

1. How can cross-cultural information help us better understand the human nature God has given to us, including our need of friendship?

2. Why did Christ select only men as His closest friends and disciples?

3. What indication is there in your life that your desire for personal privacy and freedom is stronger than your desire for community and involvement in the lives of others?

4. How could friendship receive more social recognition similar to marriage and parenting roles?

5. Suggest ways to practically apply biblical hospitality in your everyday life, and then plan to put your ideas into action.

Chapter 8
Understanding Yourself

"The better part of one's life consists of his friend-ships." *Abraham Lincoln*

"OK, I see the problem of my friendless condition and I understand the principles leading to a better life. But actually changing my behavior and thinking patterns is quite difficult." Reaching this point of awareness is the first step to improvement. Before progress occurs one must believe that progress is needed.

Acting on new knowledge frequently requires, first, the understanding of who and what we are today, and then, the unlearning, by daily application of biblical principles, of what we previously were taught. To understand ourselves is difficult. Self-examination is a personal and sometimes painful exercise. Socrates said, "Know thyself." He also said, "The unexamined life is not worth living." Most of us, however, would just as soon forego participation in objective introspection.

But there are no shortcuts to personal change and growth. Don't be discouraged. Knowledge and personal examination are not enough. Action is needed. God defines much of life as a process of becoming. We push toward the mark. We grow in grace. We begin as babes in Christ. There are no shortcuts to growth; but the process, getting from where we are to where we want to go, can be enjoyable.

Caution: Assimilating biblical principles takes time. Once a problem is identified, it is the nature of the American male to require an immediate solution. But if we fail to change at the core of our personality, our thinking will not be altered and our new behavior will be contrived. Sooner or later we will backslide into old patterns.

You can successfully apply biblical principles and thereby develop quality relationships with others. Sure it's difficult to seriously look within to see why we act and think as we do. "Am I afraid? Am I a bigot? Am I hateful? Am I impatient? Am I selfish? Am I arrogant? Am I comfortable in my self-sufficiency?" We must ask these and other personal and uncomfortable questions of ourselves, and answer them one by one, objectively in the context of our everyday lives.

Ingrained Prejudices

I attended an educational meeting last spring. Methods for educating talented and gifted children are being looked at closely within my own school corporation, so when I learned that this topic was going to be considered at one of the sessions, I was quite pleased. Arriving a few minutes early, I settled in, anticipating a useful lecture on gifted education. Sometimes we learn more than we want to about ourselves, or something different from what we expect. This was true for me in this situation.

The elementary school teacher who spoke to our group was a young, attractive, well-dressed woman. When I learned she was the speaker my initial thought was, "What could she know about gifted education at the high school and college levels?" Well, it was really too late to get up and leave; besides it would have been rude to do so.

I am glad I remained. She was intelligent and quite knowledgeable about the neglected topic of how best to teach brilliant children. Much of what she said was useful for the level of student I worked with as well.

Why then was I turned off before I gave her a chance? I always have told my children, Julie and Jason, "Don't make snap judgments, give people a chance, don't be prejudiced." And yet it was I who was prejudiced. Maybe it was because she was young—"What does she know, she's only a kid." Deep down maybe I also held a prejudice that an attractive woman is rarely very intelligent. Maybe I would have responded in the same fashion to an average-looking woman—because she was a woman. (Am I really a chauvinist?) And then there was the fact that she represented the lower elementary grades which may have affected me. Whatever the cause of my quickly formed, unfair stereotype, I was dead wrong.

What helps is to constantly ask yourself, "Why am I reacting this way toward this person?" Only when you bring your values to a conscious level will there be hope for a solution.

Many of us men must admit that we often make snap judgments and then, mentally or physically or both, we withdraw from someone who could possibly be a true source of potential friendship. We've got to break away from the temptation to rapidly form first impressions. It's of course convenient and easy to construct summary conclusions about someone, but it's both unjust and a distortion of reality.

Incidentally, first impressions, once formed, are rather difficult to change, even when confronted with new information which conflicts with your unfair stereotype. Don't do it; don't make unfair snap judgments about another person's intelligence, knowledge, character, personality, spirituality, or motives. It's wrong to do so. You may wound another person's spirit or self-confidence while, at the same time, starve yourself from the needed nutrition that comes from entering into the lives of others. The Bible very clearly states, for example in James 2, that prejudice is sin.

It's extremely difficult to uproot ingrained prejudices once established. Gordon W. Alport, in his classic work *The Nature of Prejudice,* says that once we acquire prejudices we tend unconsciously to defend them in the face of facts that contradict our beliefs.

Learning that I too was prejudiced was only part of what I learned from the teacher that hosted the gifted workshop. I had settled in my seat, and although skeptical, I was ready to listen to her speech. Soon after she began, however, she divided us into small groups. She wanted us to work together on a project that would help us learn more about gifted kids. Well, it did fulfill its intended purpose, but I learned something else as well. The women in our seminar were more eager to work together and to share ideas. I honestly felt a little uncomfortable sharing with others and depending upon others to complete the assigned activity.

Like most men I am used to working alone. We tend to believe that our greatest successes come from individual and independent efforts on some task. I remember few incidences in my college or graduate school experiences where I was really put in a situation similar to this gifted workshop where there was sharing and an effort to learn together. In my formal learning experiences I worked instead in competition with classmates.

After I got beyond my uncomfortable feeling in the

small group to which I was assigned, I thoroughly enjoyed the learning experience. The adage, "If you want a job done right, do it yourself," is not always true. We must not shrink from social, religious, or work-related activities that bring us into contact with other people.

Isolation in Moderation

Self-imposed psychological and/or physical isolation is good only in moderation. Don't try to do everything by yourself. The author of the following humorous account is unknown. I'm sure you'll agree that it illustrates that there are times we need and should accept the help of others.

Dear Sir:

I am writing in response to your request for more information concerning Block #11 on the insurance form which asks for "cause of injuries" wherein I put "Trying to do the job alone." You said you needed more information so I trust the following will be sufficient.

I am a bricklayer by trade and on the date of injuries I was working alone laying brick around the top of a four-story building when I realized that I had about 500 pounds of brick left over. Rather than carry the bricks down by hand, I decided to put them into a barrel and lower them by a pulley which was fastened to the top of the building. I secured the end of the rope at ground level and went up to the top of the building and loaded the bricks into the barrel and swung the barrel out with the bricks in it. I then went down and untied the rope, holding it securely to insure the slow descent of the barrel.

As you will note on Block #6 of the insurance form, I weigh 145 pounds. Due to my shock at being jerked off the ground so swiftly, I lost my presence of mind and forgot to let go of the rope. Between the second and third floors I met the barrel coming down. This accounts for the bruises and lacerations on my upper body.

Regaining my presence of mind again, I held tightly to the rope and proceeded rapidly up the side of the building not stopping until my right hand was jammed in the pulley. This accounts for the broken thumb.

Despite the pain, I retained my presence of mind and held tightly to the rope. At approximately the same time, however, the barrel of bricks hit the ground and the bottom fell out of the barrel. Devoid of the weight of the bricks, the barrel now weighed about 50 pounds. I again refer you to Block #6 and my weight.

As you would guess, I began a rapid descent. In the vicinity of the second floor I met the barrel coming up. This explains the injuries to my legs and lower body. Slowed only slightly, I continued my descent landing on the pile of bricks. This accounts for my sprained back and internal injuries.

I am sorry to report, however, that at this point, I again lost my presence of mind and let go of the rope, and as you can imagine, the empty barrel crashed down on me. This accounts for my head injuries.

I trust this answers your concern. Please know that I am finished "Trying to do the job alone."

The first time I heard this list of woes by the insured, I just howled. It's funny to me because it contains much truth for my own life, and I bet for yours too. If we would just reach out and ask for help we would avoid many difficulties such as the man in the insurance report had, and have more fun and accomplish more in the process.

One man told me, "No way, you don't teach an old dog new tricks. I've been this way too long to change now." I answered him, "Your problem isn't your inability to change but rather a fear of the unknown. You're afraid to change." What will people think? What if I fail? People may think I'm pushy. I may be snubbed if I reach out to others. People might be suspect of my motives.

Facing Our Fears

During the Great Depression Franklin D. Roosevelt said, "The only thing we have to far is fear itself." Our fears, often unconscious, tend to paralyze us, preventing the possibility of change. "God hath not given us the spirit of fear; but . . . of a sound mind" (2 Tim. 1:7, *KJV*). We have, therefore, the ability to face up to our fears and to deal with them rationally, logically, prayerfully, as we lean on the support of God and those who love us. Fear, squarely faced, tends to ebb in significance. In Bunyan's nineteenth-century classic *Pilgrim's Progress*, Christian's path was beset by alarming shapes that scuttled about in the shifting mists. These sinister monsters proved to be tiny creatures unable to hurt anyone. You need to realize that your fear is unnecessary. To paraphrase Philippians 4:6, "Don't be uptight about this. Rather ask God to help you with your fears."

Break through to other men in short small stages. As you do, your fears will ebb. Explore ideas and, later, feelings with other men. Ask their opinions and be willing to share a few of your own. By working with others, by asking their thinking on a topic you send forth the subtle message that you recognize and respect them as individuals. William James the influential psychologist of the early 1900s said, "The deepest principle of man is the craving to be appreciated."

When I was teaching high school and college social studies classes I required that students prepare a research paper dealing with a problem or issue within American society. Part of the assignment was to interview two individuals who were directly involved in some way with the subject matter of the paper. To be sure, this assignment was not often received with enthusiasm. Students feared that the men and women they wanted to interview would resent giving them time. These students were also afraid they would ask dumb questions.

We discovered that, with few exceptions, those interviewed were very willing to talk with students. Some even called me to offer to speak to the entire class or just to say thanks for the opportunity to share. Those interviewed were glad to take the time to share because someone asked their opinion.

The students sent thank-you notes and reported enthusiastically that it was a good experience. We as men, similar to these kids, need to ask questions and take an interest in others. Again, fear is unnecessary. Usually you'll be pleasantly surprised when you befriend others.

Importance of Touch

Although an abundance of research exists that men need both to give and to receive physical affection, rarely does a man express his feelings physically. We do not touch. Touching of any kind implies sex to most men. If they are not engaged in heated combat on the football field, or engrossed in sexual intercourse, American men will not touch other humans, especially men. We are afraid. We have been conditioned to believe that expressing emotions is wrong.

Andrew M. Greely, in his book *The Friendship Game*, argues that fear is the major barrier to friendship. I must agree. Even within the church we see people sitting together—alone. We smile, we might even say hello, but we don't know one another. This solitary worship is easy, for it demands nothing of us. How different the contemporary American church is from the ideal established by Jesus. In John 13, Jesus says that people will know that we belong to Him if we have love for each other. Over the past decade or so, several evangelicals have attempted to recapture the caring, open, sharing relationships within the body of Christians. Leaders in this relational theology movement are, among others, Bruce Larson (*Dare to Live, Living on the Growing Edge*) and Keith Miller (*Taste of New Wine*). Don't blame others if things are not as you wish. As the Bell ad says, "Reach out and touch someone."

Before beginning a recent Saturday morning shopping venture, my family and I had breakfast in an Indianapolis restaurant. While we were eating and building up the courage to face what seemed like an endless list of retail stores, Sue Ann drew my attention to something unusual. Two cars had pulled up together. A family of five or six piled out of each car. Everyone began talking to each other. There were smiles and handshakes all around. This was a pleasant sight, but not all that unusual. As we were enjoying what must have been a family reunion, two of the men actually hugged each other unashamedly, and then walked into the restaurant continuing to talk with arms around each other's shoulders.

We finished our breakfast. Before leaving I couldn't resist the temptation to find out why these two men were so affectionate. Not surprisingly, they were glad to talk with me but had not thought much about the showing of their feelings. The men were brothers who had been raised by an affectionate mother who had not instructed her sons to internalize all of their feelings.

Maybe you didn't have such an upbringing and still keep most or all of your feelings to yourself. It's never too late to change. Whom do you care about? Do they know how you feel about them? It's high time you tell them before it's too late. Some men, due to childhood training, simply cannot physically show how they feel, especially to another man. Each of us, however, has the ability and the need to tell other people how we feel about them. Sure you can be discreet, and the time should be appropriate and non-embarrassing, but the point is, don't let a relationship suffer or even die because of poor communication.

Be Strong!

Sue and I were married on a muggy August afternoon in South Bend, Indiana in 1965. From that beginning and even before, during our engagement, we had talked about how many children we wanted for our family. Did we want a boy first or a girl? We decided it didn't really matter. Then we discussed how many did we want and how far apart we would space them. If this wasn't naive enough, we also talked of what month we should conceive. If she became pregnant in—say—September our baby would be born in the spring, which we thought would be an ideal time.

Well, so much for well-intentioned plans. The years came and went. We remained childless, but not for a lack of trying. We saw a urologist and a fertility specialist. Sue was prescribed a fertility drug which she took faithfully for three or four years. Still no baby.

We lived in a young married, family-oriented neighborhood. Sue became bored and even angry with the incessant talk about children and birth and labor experiences. Late at night my wife would cry. Her tears expressed her desire for motherhood. Being a normal man, I felt uncomfortable when on occasion she would share her feelings and express her emotion. As I think back, I believe I was actually uncomfortable with my feelings rather than Sue's. How do you act? What do you say or do? I guess I wanted to appear strong when I too was hurting.

Following much prayer we agreed (it was easy for me) that Sue would undergo an operation. It was like an answer to prayer. Sue became pregnant a few months later. It seemed so right. We had been married over seven years, had worked as youth leaders in the church and wanted young people of our own. Besides we informed God during our innumerable petitions that we had indeed learned the patience He must obviously intend for us to acquire.

All that waiting and frustration were now behind us, or so we thought. It was the middle of the night when Sue awakened me. "Something is wrong. We had better call the physician." The rest of the night and following two days were spent in the hospital. We lost our child whom we had grown to love and anticipate during his five months of development in Sue's body.

I didn't cry. An attending physician told me, "Be strong so you can help your wife. She's emotional right now." But it was I rather than my wife who was acting abnormally. She was feeling and expressing the grief and sense of loss in a normal fashion. Sue found it difficult to understand why I didn't cry. I knew the Bible doesn't tell us it is wrong to sorrow. After all Jesus wept openly and unashamedly at the grave of His friend Lazarus.

I returned home to pack a bag for Sue and to make a few phone calls. It was at home in total solitude that I finally wept. Today I know those tears were good for me and would have been better if they had been shared with Sue, for they helped to release the emotional buildup of anger, resentment, and sense of loss. But at the time I felt ashamed. I called my mother and the strong male image I had wished to maintain simply collapsed when I finally cried.

Sue convalesced at home for several days. It was during this time that I was finally able to reveal my emotions by talking and crying with Sue and planning a week's trip away together. This sharing and planning did much to begin the healing of our hearts. I, as much as Sue, needed to talk about what happened.

People mean well but the comments we received were unsettling. Some Christians would, with little emotional energy or empathy, quote Romans 8:28 or tell us since it's not God's will that you have a real or natural child maybe you should consider adoption. Craig Massey, our pastor while we lived in Des Plaines, Illinois learned of our situation and wrote us a letter which I have saved. He begins the letter with, "How sad I was to hear of the departure of one you never saw but one whom you loved." We still appreciate the tenderness he conveyed by his letter.

Another Christian told us the baby was not a person yet. Psalm 139 was so comforting at this point, for we knew our child was indeed precious to God. We knew that the baby was not an accident and that his death did not take God by surprise. Excerpts from Psalm 139 read as follows.

For you created my inmost being;
  you knit me together in my mother's womb.
I praise you because I am fearfully and wonderfully made;
  your works are wonderful, I know that full well.
My frame was not hidden from you
  when I was made in the secret place.
When I was woven together in the depths of the earth,
  your eyes saw my unformed body (vv. 13-16).

(If you're interested in this topic, two new books are helpful for couples who have lost a baby. Barb Berg has written *Nothing to Cry About* and Dr. Larry Pepper's book is *Motherhood and Mourning*.)

We need to learn to grieve and to share our grief with others. If we fail to express our emotional feelings with those we care for I'm convinced our lives will be lonely and possibly shortened. And we probably won't be much fun or comfort to others either.

Purpose for Living

At the end of a long life the famous Swiss psychiatrist Carl Jung said that "the central neurosis of our time is emptiness." In the play *Death of a Salesman*, Willy Loman examines his many lonely years of existence and concludes that life is meaningless. For many life is empty.

This need not be your situation if you are in proper harmony with both your Creator and your fellow humans. Victor Frankl found in his study of World War II concentration camp prisoners, that those who survived had a couple of things in common: (1) They stayed alive because of a purpose for living; (2) they had loved ones they wanted to see and love again. You can discover and develop your purpose for living through a commitment to Jesus Christ and by study and application of biblical principles in all areas of life. And you can express your love and share your life with those who are close to you.

You Can Change!

God's help and your own resolve provide the best combination known to man. Your own determination and inner strength are more powerful than you might at first realize. The Lord has given each of us various gifts and talents that we are to use. D.L. Moody once said that if your house is burning, don't pray about it, put the fire out. There is truth to the criticism that some Christians act so heavenly they are of no earthly good. It is not a contradiction to depend upon God and yourself at the same time. You realize that God is the ultimate source of your strength, and at the same time, that you are personally responsible for what you do and say.

You must believe in yourself and in your ability to change. Don't meditate on past defeats as many men do. You can't do anything if you believe you can't. Even in areas of your life where you have experienced failure the correct response is not, "I can't do this." With this attitude you'll *never* be able to do whatever "this" might be. A more appropriate response is, "With God's help, I'll turn this failure into victory." In the book *How to Be Your Own Best Friend* the authors suggest, "If we all just kept on doing exactly what we've done up to now, people would never change, and people are changing all the time. That's what growth is—doing what you've never done before."[21]

On my desk at home I have a card which reads, "You Are What You Do, Not What You Say You'll Do." This reminder helps me to overcome one of my persistent weaknesses—procrastination. What are the roadblocks in your life that are preventing you from fully participating in a more useful, abundant life? What patterns of thought or behavior now separate you from applying biblical principles of friendship?

One secret of success in changing long-standing patterns is to, first, concentrate on specific items that need change, and, second, to strive for small improvement. The trip of a thousand miles begins with a single step. Begin small. As you create and achieve realistic short-range goals, sooner or later you'll enjoy significant improvement.

What is in your life that now prevents you from making biblical principles and positive personality traits part of your life? Figure 1 (see p. 132) shows a check sheet that should help you identify problems you should work on.

You have selected certain items in figure 1 that you feel are definite problems in the way you think or behave. It is in these very areas that you need to focus your attention. For each item that you said was serious ask, "Why is this a problem? Where am I right now with this problem? What is my goal? And how do I get from where I am to where I want to be?" Set goals for yourself and list in small manageable steps how you'll accomplish the desired end result.

In the final analysis you cannot say that you are what you are because society has taught you to be macho, or your parents raised you incorrectly, or you were converted too early or too late in life, or you're a man, or because of any other external factor. To allow yourself to be controlled by external variables is to become little more than a robot. *You are what you are because you want to be what you are.* You are the person in control of your life. The Freudians have given us much insight into the human mind but they err on this critical point. You are responsible to God and man for your behavior, because you are relatively free to act as you please. We are not puppets on strings, totally controlled by social and psychological forces as Peter Berger argues eloquently in his *Invitation to Sociology.*

Edward O. Wilson in his controversial book *Social Biology* goes even further claiming that our behavior is the result of how we were raised *and* how our genes were programmed. In virtually every field of social science today, and now too in the natural sciences, there is a view of man as machine. Machines of course are not responsible for their behavior and are useful only if they can produce something valued by the culture. Machines are disposable and lack morals or intrinsic value.

This is not the Bible's view of man. We are not a *tab-*

ula rasa or a mindless lump of clay that is molded by others. How much control do I really have over my own life? Can I change on my own or do I need counseling to improve my patterns of living? In some cases we can engage in self-examination on a solo basis. Self-reflection and contemplation are always helpful. But many men need the added insights, understanding, and objectivity that can be provided only by an outsider such as a close friend, wife, or even a counselor.

When I mention therapy, what comes to mind? Most evangelicals turn off when they hear the term, associating it with Freudian psychology and psychoanalysis. John Warwick Montgomery says we are morally offended by Sigmund Freud's explaining God away as a father figure, as atheistic and materialistic. Christians explain Freud away as a product of his own neurosis. The man had serious emotional problems himself (as did his disciple Carl Jung) and admitted he had little interest in helping suffering humanity, only in understanding it. There exists a danger in accepting without examination the tenets of modern psychology.

What does one do following a rejection of the beliefs of psychoanalysis? After all, emotional pain is a real phenomenon. Fortunately, most emotional problems can be alleviated if someone is willing to invest both concern and time in our well-being. O. Quentin Hyder, M.D., says,

This is the key to good psychotherapy and counseling—to care, to really care, and to let the sufferer know that you care. If more Christians made themselves available in this way to help the weaker brother and sister in need when the troubles first started, there would be far fewer numbers of them having to go later for professional help. The burden of my message is that caring Christians can significantly contribute to the mental and emotional health of their fellow church members and Christian friends. To do so we must make ourselves available and give time and our own emotional energies and resources to succor those in need.[22]

People with serious adjustment problems should consult an evangelical pastor, one who knows of biblically-based professional counselors. I would also suggest reading William Glasser, *Reality Therapy*; Alber Ellis, *A New Guide to Rational Living*; Paul Tournier, *The Healing of Persons*; C.S. Lewis, *The Problem of Pain*; Cecil Osborne, *The Art of Understanding Your Mate*.[23]

In most cases you can change without the use of professional help. Christ can free you from your old negative life-style patterns (2 Cor. 5:17) and provide you with what is good for both you and those around you (Gal. 5:22,23; 2 Pet. 1:5-7). You are the person in control of your life. With God at your side, begin now to change how you think and how you behave. Don't put it off. No day is a bad day to begin.

Our greatest problem is not other people but rather ourselves. Remember the Pogo quote at the beginning of chapter 2—"We have met the enemy, and he is us"? In the Galatian letter (5:17) Paul records that for the Christian, human nature and one's spiritual nature are in dire contradiction. What we need is help. Good intentions, no matter how pure, like New Year's resolutions, rarely result in long-term changed attitudes and behavior. You need your own resolve and dedication to be sure; but one additional step is also needed—without the support of God, changes, if they occur at all, are usually cosmetic as well as short-lived.

"Let God change you inwardly" (Rom. 12:2, *TEV*). *Phillips* translates this verse, "Let God remold your minds from within."

Discussion Questions

1. What roadblocks prevent you from making friends?

2. How did you do on the friendship inventory? What small steps can you begin to work on in the problem areas?

3. Do hugging, crying, or other outward expressions of affection make you feel uncomfortable? Why?

4. In what ways are you like the bricklayer who attempted to do the job alone? Why is the story funny?

5. Do you enjoy the daily process of personal growth or are you living in either the past or the future?

6. What causes prejudice and what can be done to prevent or remove it? Has prejudice hindered you from forming friendships with certain individuals?

7. At what point should a man seek outside help to solve psychological and/or spiritual problems?

Friendship Inventory

	No problem with me	Some improvement needed here	This is a major problem
CHRIST-CENTERED			
I'm concerned with the spirituality of the men I know.	☐	☐	☐
I'm able to talk about Christ and the Bible with friends.	☐	☐	☐
I pray with and for my friends.	☐	☐	☐
The activities I share with friends are wholesome.	☐	☐	☐
I regularly include God in my thoughts and plans.	☐	☐	☐
COVENANT			
I remember important anniversaries and celebrate them with letters, cards or calls.	☐	☐	☐
I'm not afraid to risk being rejected by reaching out to another.	☐	☐	☐
I have told my friends that they are important to me.	☐	☐	☐
I make every effort to try to heal a strained or broken relationship.	☐	☐	☐
My friends know that I honor my commitments.	☐	☐	☐
FAITHFULNESS			
My friends can count on me.	☐	☐	☐
I can keep a confidence.	☐	☐	☐
I take full responsibility for what I do and say.	☐	☐	☐
Circumstances affect my consistency.	☐	☐	☐
SOCIAL INVOLVEMENT			
I enjoy making new friends—I ask people questions to learn more about them.	☐	☐	☐
I care enough about new acquaintances to greet them warmly.	☐	☐	☐
I don't begrudge the giving of my time or money when I see a needy person or cause.	☐	☐	☐
I plant shade trees under which I know I'll never sit (I'm not selfish).	☐	☐	☐
I'm a good neighbor—I do not criticize others (like the Good Samaritan).	☐	☐	☐
I am not prejudiced. I do not discriminate against individuals who are of a different race, ethnic group, religion or social class.	☐	☐	☐

CANDOR

I speak the truth in love.	☐	☐	☐
I am honest in my relationships.	☐	☐	☐
I'm not defensive if a friend talks about a problem in my life.	☐	☐	☐
I can ask for help if I'm in need.	☐	☐	☐

RESPECT

I really believe God loves each individual.	☐	☐	☐
I am tactful, considerate, and do not take advantage of close friends.	☐	☐	☐
I express gratitude when I've been helped by someone.	☐	☐	☐
I have a deep-seated belief in the inherent worth of myself and others.	☐	☐	☐
I respect the right of each of my friends to be different from me (I respect their opinions).	☐	☐	☐

ACCEPTANCE

I know God has forgiven me.	☐	☐	☐
I am not judgmental of the behavior and thinking of others. (I am tolerant.)	☐	☐	☐
Material things or status are not important in my relationships.	☐	☐	☐
I look for the good in others and minimize their faults.	☐	☐	☐
I express precise and honest appreciations.	☐	☐	☐
I don't hold grudges.	☐	☐	☐

EMPATHY

People I know experience God's love through me.	☐	☐	☐
I sincerely try to understand how other people feel and think (I invest the time needed to accomplish this).	☐	☐	☐
I do not force my views on other people.	☐	☐	☐
I treat other people as equals.	☐	☐	☐

LISTENING

I look for the feeling in people's words.	☐	☐	☐
I don't talk too much or interrupt people when they talk.	☐	☐	☐
I ask men questions about their own lives.	☐	☐	☐
I listen alertly and avoid distractions.	☐	☐	☐
I take the time needed to listen to others.	☐	☐	☐

LOYALTY

I am dependable and consistent.	☐	☐	☐
I am not a fair-weather friend.	☐	☐	☐
I keep in touch with friends now separated from me by miles.	☐	☐	☐

SELF-DISCLOSURE

I do not try to act like someone I'm not. (I am genuine.)	☐	☐	☐
My friends and I confide in each other.	☐	☐	☐

I'm willing to reveal a weakness or ask for help from a friend. ☐ ☐ ☐

I don't fear sharing my emotions. ☐ ☐ ☐

COMPROMISE

I don't have to always have things my way. ☐ ☐ ☐

I do not expect my friends to be perfect (friends without faults don't exist). ☐ ☐ ☐

When wrong I admit it (I also say I'm sorry). ☐ ☐ ☐

I deal with conflicting ideas with reason and understanding. ☐ ☐ ☐

I do not have a competitive, win-or-lose orientation that makes life a succession of contests. ☐ ☐ ☐

I do have the capacity to adapt to new conditions in a spirit of cooperation. ☐ ☐ ☐

Figure 1

Chapter 9

Confronting American Culture

"Do not conform any longer to the pattern of this world, but be transformed by the renewing of your mind. Then you will be able to test and approve what God's will is." *Romans 12:2*

How has American culture contributed to our becoming friendless?

During the nineteenth century the United States was mainly a rural and agricultural nation. Most families lived on farms in sparsely populated areas. Work and other activities were done together by all members of the family. The wife, husband, and children all shared the tasks of producing what the family itself consumed.

As the country developed into an industrial nation, sex roles became more rigid. Usually it was the man who left the home and the farm to earn a living in town. Children left home to attend school. Women remained in the home to care for small children and household duties. Roles became more sharply defined. What it meant to be a man or a woman became more narrowly defined. But during World War II hundreds of thousands of American women left home to enter the factories of America in an attempt to help with the war effort.

Following the war, for economic and social reasons, many women remained in the work force, and many men married and went to college on the G.I. bill. With wives working full time and husbands in school, less of a stigma existed for males who shared domestic chores of laundry, shopping, and cleaning. Our culture began to change its definition again of what is male or what is female behavior. But we have not yet redefined maleness to allow men to express their feelings and fears and therefore conform to biblical norms. Far from it. For example we're still suspicious of a man who spends "too much" time caring for children. Nor can one be too understanding or too emotional if he wants to avoid raised eyebrows.

Frontier Ethic

Despite the significant changes in this and the last century, many men still adhere to what I would call a frontier ethic which is a throwback to the eighteenth and nineteenth centuries. They still exalt the image of the powerful autonomous men of the West such as Daniel Boone, Kit Carson or Davy Crockett, albeit in altered form to fit the twentieth century. The illusion of *Gunsmoke's* Matt Dillon may have evolved to become Officer McClain of *McClain's Law*, the most recent TV show which features James Arness. The setting may have changed from a frontier town to a modern city, but Arness in the new role maintains a frontier masculinity— although it may be more subdued.

In the shoot-out at the OK Corral one could not afford to be second-best. On the frontier combating the elements, starvation, disease, wild animals, and Indians, one had to always win. First place was all that was available. To lose was to die.

Writing in the late nineteenth century, progressive historian Frederick J. Turner argued in his very famous essay *The Significance of the Frontier in American History* that the frontier has uniquely shaped the American character. The frontier worked to produce tough, industrious, self-reliant Americans who struggled to overcome the hazards of the wilderness.

While the frontier disappeared nearly a century ago, many still cling to a frontier mentality. The frontier behavior and thinking which served earlier generations in their struggles with physical survival is an anachronism today. We still feel that finishing first is vital to our masculinity, to our emotional survival. Vince Lombardi's, "Winning isn't everything it's the only thing" illustrates this belief. During the 1970s the Minnesota Vikings finished many football seasons by winning play-off championships, but were relegated by the press to the loser category since they failed to win "the big one." The big one of course is the Super Bowl, currently America's most important annual pageant. The San Francisco Giants got the same treatment in the late fifties and sixties. The Dallas Cowboys also had a great string of play-off victories in the 1960s. What was said of this winning team? They too couldn't win the big one. We're told that heated competition makes winners, and so it does. But it makes many more non-winners. And even the winners are losers in the minds of some because they can't win the so-called big one.

Neil Armstrong was the first man on the moon. Who was second? Who was vice-president (second place) in the administrations of Washington, Jefferson, Lincoln, Wilson, Roosevelt or Kennedy? Even in more recent days, many would be hard pressed to identify the V.P. in the Nixon, Ford, Carter or Reagan administrations.

We're told, although incorrectly, that Columbus was first to discover America. Who was second? The second man to fly solo across the Atlantic was as daring as Charles Lindbergh, but no one ever hears of him.

Might makes right today as well as it did on the frontier. Money and power make even a sleazy character like Al Capone important. The frontier ethic of being first at all costs is only one anachronistic legacy that still plagues our culture's view of the way American males must perform in the 1980s.

Social Darwinism

In the 1880s a new philosophy was popularized, partially to justify an emerging rootlessness in business, but also to explain why only a few were winners in the competitive game of life. Those with great wealth needed some way philosophically to numb the guilt they felt when they surveyed the desperate poverty that multitudes were forced to endure.

Rather than attempt to create a more equitable means to distribute income, many of the rich sought a system to explain why the poor were themselves to blame for their misery. Another philosophy was needed to blame the victim for his condition and thus remove personal responsibilities and need for correct action.

Using the biological theories developed by Charles Darwin in the 1850s, the English philosopher Herbert Spencer, and others, developed the idea of "social darwinism." Now one could justify and explain away the disparity of very rich and very poor as the workings of the iron laws of nature. The rich, and many of the poor themselves, believed or at least supported the argument that fixed laws of nature existed to guide human conduct. Rather than beneficent, nature became vicious as survival of the fittest was the law for human behavior as well as for the animal world. The poor and handicapped were therefore viewed as unfit and expendable as nature attempted to better each species.

Therefore, if you had great wealth it was not due to your parents or a gift from God, but rather because you were superior to other creatures and were meant to lord it over lesser men as some powerful animals control or destroy their prey. Natural selection, not divine providence, reigns supreme.

With this thinking the American psyche drifted far from the Christian world view which, illustrated in Jesus, elevated the values of gentleness, concern, and sensitivity for others. Rather than destroy or explain away the weak, Jesus was compassionate and offered help. His discussion of the Good Samaritan will forever stand as a beacon of hope for the downtrodden and also as a challenge for those who have the capacity to reach out to others less fortunate. He came to serve others (Matt. 20:28). Jesus had time for people, even so-called unimportant people like the woman at the well. He touched people like the leper (Luke 5:12-13) and wasn't too concerned if others thought He was doing the wrong thing according to the cultural values of the moment. And He wanted to spend time with children (Mark 10:13-16). These traits are not exactly valued in our contemporary culture.

The narrow American belief in the virtues of self-reliance, strength, courage, independence, and finishing first at the exclusion of other values and realities has taken a heavy toll upon modern man. Popular author Horatio Alger perpetuated the myth of the self-made man in his widely read novels of several decades ago. As a result the multitudes who fail to finish first, who fail to become corporate presidents or champions in a multitude of ways, are left with feelings of failure. Ironically perhaps, Alger himself is an example of the failure to live up to the American dream, as his own life was a personal disaster.

What is not mentioned in the novels or in the cultural ethics is that men with power and money tend to pass on their money and power to their children. And children of poor parents tend to produce children who grow up poor despite a desire to rise above conditions. This is not always true, however; real opportunities do exist in this great country. We must remember that America has a comfortable middle class that includes the grandchildren and great-grandchildren of lower classes that migrated to America at the turn of the century. Most of those who have acquired money and power, however, are white, protestant and from Northwest Europe.

A few people began to challenge the cultural illusion during the Great Depression when very able and willing men were unable to find work of any sort, much less the great jobs associated with money and power. They were not the sole determiners of their destiny. Impersonal enemies, such as economic conditions, prevented people from being self-reliant.

Using popular symbolisms of physical strength, David in Psalm 147 illustrates how the Lord is not impressed with the autonomous strength-myth that is ingrained in the American mind. David records, "His pleasure is not in the strength of the horse, nor his delight in the legs of a man; the Lord delights in those who fear him, who put their hope in his unfailing love" (vv. 10,11). David is telling us not to depend solely upon ourselves for strength. He says, The Lord God is my strength.

American men, victimized by our culture, have a difficult time buying into the idea of leaning on another person for strength, least of all God. It goes against the grain of our culture. In discussing this, Greg Risber commented, "John Wayne who embodied the ideal man, both on and off the screen, wouldn't say, 'I'm scared but let's attack.' He says, 'Let's kill the s.o.b.'s.' " Mr. Risber belongs to the Chicago Men's Gathering (CMG) a discussion group of men that feel they've lived for 30 or 40 years in a man's world that seems obsolete, unworkable, and undesirable.

Christians must reject our culture's benign neglect— or worse, its hostility toward those Americans who are weak or handicapped—and ask themselves, What do I as a Christian man owe people who are not as well off as I am?

Signs of Civilization

During the nine years that I taught anthropology classes I would ask students to define what is an advanced civilization. Almost every student would mention countries or cultures which had achieved a technological superiority over their contemporaries. Like most people, the students invariably associated technological advance as an indication of civilization. Most often mentioned was America's ability to put Neil Armstrong on the moon in 1969. Even the Quaker president of the United States at the time, Richard Nixon, referred to the lunar landing as "the greatest event in all of world history," therefore superseding creation, the birth, death and resurrection of Christ, the triumph of forming democracies, the invention of vaccines, or the tragedy of genocide or barbarism. The moon landing was a mechanical triumph of the highest order, but what of our need for triumph in the spiritual and human levels?

Francis Schaeffer and many others feel that the advance of technology has been a mixed blessing. While providing comfort and convenience it also has worked to separate us from one another. Dr. Schaeffer points out that in years gone by, in the Swiss mountains, women worked with their husbands all day in the fields and then slept with them all night. Today men spend their time with tractors. This is not to debate the importance of machinery and the advantages it yields, but only to say that specialization of labor and technology may cut down the amount and quality of time we spend with loved ones. We continue to sacrifice friendship, fellowship, and community for material things.

Scripture does not agree with this philosophy. Paul, in 2 Corinthians 4:18, lays out the criterion for civilization, and the inadequacy of material things: "So we fix our eyes not on what is seen, but on what is unseen. For what is seen is temporary, but what is unseen is eternal."

No, the mark of civilization is not material or technological advancement. Nazi Germany in the 1930s and 1940s killed millions of people efficiently and rapidly with some of the most sophisticated technology of those decades; and yet by anyone's definition the Nazis must be viewed as uncivilized.

The mark of civilization, I told my students, is how individuals and entire people treat the weak, those less fortunate, who lack power and influence. The weak are the defenseless—those who lack strength in body, mind, or spirit. Men are not to dominate or even sideline these people but are to emulate the servant's heart of Jesus. In the nineteenth and early twentieth centuries it was largely the Christian community, not the social darwinists, who worked for the removal of slavery, child labor practices, inhumane prisons, and mental institutions.

Romans 14 and 15 calls us to be active in our community. We are to be involved in helping those who have real needs which they themselves are unable to satisfy. Deuteronomy 15:7,8 reads, "If there is among you a poor man . . . you shall open your hand to him, and lend him sufficient for his need" (*RSV*). First Timothy 6:18 instructs us "to do good, to be rich in good deeds, and to be generous and willing to share."

Late in the nineteenth century Ferdinand Tornies, a German sociologist, contrasted and generalized two distinct kinds of societies. One is *gemeinschaft* which means commitment to community, sense of belonging, moral stability, tradition, sharing of attitudes, intimacy and extended kinship, fixed status, and shared sacred values.

In sharp contrast, *gesellschaft* loosely translates as a group created for a special purpose, like a business that is voluntary and established to pursue self-interest. People freely join this type of society and see it as a practical way of reaching or achieving certain goals. This corresponds with American men who learn early in life that they are to concentrate on the accomplishing and the pursuing of goals, and not to be too concerned with relating to people.

And yet if given the opportunity to choose from either freedom and convenience or community and intimacy it would be a difficult choice for most of us. We enjoy our privacy even with the knowledge that with solitude can come loneliness. Ralph Keyes in his 1973 book *We the Lonely People* says that above all else we Americans value mobility, privacy and convenience. And it is these very traits that are at the source of our lack of community. Of these three, privacy is our most cherished value. But it has not always been this way. Keyes reminds us, "Privacy as an ideal, even as a concept, is relatively modern. Marshall McLuhan says it took the invention of print to tear man from his tribes and plant the dream of isolation in his brain. Historian Jacob Burchhardt says that before the Renaissance, Western man was barely aware of himself as an individual. Mostly he drew identity from membership in groups—family, tribe, church, guild."[24]

Francis Schaeffer in his important book *How Shall We Then Live?*, argues that one of our most precious values in late twentieth-century America is the desire to be left alone. We are a private people. Alvin Toffler argued more than a decade ago in *Future Shock* that we can be self-sufficient as individuals. Therefore we don't need other people as previous generations did to get through life on a day-to-day basis. The introduction of time- and labor-saving technology has reduced our need to depend upon others to help and respond to daily problems. Television alone, of course, has done much to undermine interpersonal communication.

This slide towards a *gesellschaft* culture is received with mixed feelings. Vance Packard has written that our culture, with its obsession with mobility and privacy, has produced *A Nation of Strangers*. Commenting on the stress of moving, Suzanne Gordon, author of *Lonely in America*, says she wishes she lived in a simple Chinese village where nothing changes and you know everyone from birth to death.

Mobility in the 1980s may be slowing, with more people refusing job transfers coupled with the instability of the real estate industry. But geographical movement remains substantial and we remain, as a culture, devoted to privacy and autonomy.

It need not be this way. Frustration and a feeling of hopelessness present us with an important cultural dilemma. Rather than wring our hands and talk about how good it used to be, we can today make changes in our own personal lives which will directly affect those we know, and through them we can change our cultural values. Yes, our society is fluid and dynamic and is capable of change. Indeed we have witnessed in our own lifetime more change than our ancestors experienced over several generations. Some of these changes have been good, while some aspects have been destructive.

Change is possible. We see it every day of our lives.

Therefore we can introduce biblical principles into our culture and expect to see success. Our offer of friendships, our opening up to others, can be an important solace at a time when other traditional institutions are in a state of decline. Marriage, community, and the church—in many cases—no longer provide the intimacy we all need.

To begin to confront seriously the non-biblical male values of American culture we need first to define clearly a cross-cultural masculinity that is based on Scripture.

Biblical Christian Masculinity

We need a broader definition of what it means to be masculine in the American culture. Rather than spend our time criticizing non-biblical, macho life-styles, we should rather go on the offensive by providing our family, friends, co-workers, and everyone we meet a masculinity that conforms to biblical principles.

American people are hurting and lonely and, according to Daniel Yankelovich in his book *New Rulers*, people long for connectedness and commitment. Yankelovich believes the me-first strategy is losing appeal as people hunger for deeper, more sustained, committed relationships.

Social scientists such as Thorstein Veblen, C.W. Mills, and Erich Fromm have told us throughout this century that we are living in a culture that is both materialist and consumption oriented. Men possess a materialistic view of both men and women: women are viewed one-dimensionally as sex objects; men are viewed as objects to be manipulated toward one's own selfish end.

It is time for Christians to work to liberate men from destructive definitions of masculinity which prevent the development of healthy interpersonal relationships. Call this a man's liberation movement if you like. The fact is we need a change. For committed Christians, America is a fertile field. We can be influential in the lives of others as we relate to people holistically and live a masculinity that is biblical rather than American.

Dr. Gary Collins of Trinity Seminary says that to be truly masculine is to be a follower and imitator of Jesus Christ. Christ is our great example (1 Pet. 2:21). Dr. Collins lists several Christlike characteristics which we must emulate. Christ was:

1. Dependent upon God for daily guidance, frequently at prayer and thoroughly familiar with the Scriptures

2. Intolerant of sin and a firm defender of justice

3. Compassionate and not afraid to show His feelings

4. Knowledgeable of events around Him, concerned about the poor and needy, helpful in alleviating suffering, sensitive to others and willing to tolerate personality differences

5. Characterized by love, joy, peace, patience, kindness, goodness, faithfulness, gentleness, and self-control.[25]

This masculinity that uses Jesus as its example affirms that men are able to be warm, loving, caring, open, sensitive creatures. This masculinity rejects the narrow or rigid traditional and often destructive manly role which demands that we always be tough, aggressive, and unfeeling. This masculinity puts into practice both the biblical principles of friendships from chapter 4 and the personality traits discussed in chapter 5.

God's ways may not be our culture's ways. In Luke 16:19-31 Jesus tells a parable about a man who during his lifetime had accumulated both wealth and power. In our American culture I'm sure we would call him a success. But at what cost? The man was selfish and had no concern for the needs of those in poverty. In the historical account of Luke 16, Jesus said the poor man who was neglected went to heaven while the rich and callous man ended up in hell.

The application of biblical knowledge and principles can change not only your life and the lives of those around you but can extend also to the larger culture. It seems to me that we are missing a golden opportunity in this generation to really help individuals see the bankruptcy of much that is contemporary culture. What is highly valued within our culture may well be detestable to God (Luke 16:15), but not because He doesn't want us to enjoy life. On the contrary, the Bible teaches that God wants us to live life to the fullest. To accomplish this we must live within and in accordance with certain given physical, psychological, and moral laws or principles—all given to us by God Himself in the Bible.

What we perceive through a "glass darkly" to be gold, silver, and precious stones may actually be wood, hay, stubble. To positively influence the lives of others at this time in our nation's history we must be able to distinguish between culture and Christian faith.

Vernon C. Grounds, former president of Conservative Baptist Seminary in Denver, reminds us that, to God, successful people in history like Jesus, Paul, Peter, and Stephen, are usually in conflict with their culture. Our culture has little time for the criteria God has established for us in our dealings with others. Dr. Grounds and Dr. Collins agree that God's measure of a man is Christlike love (1 Cor. 13:1-3) which produces a servant's heart and behavior (Matt. 20:25-27). This is a far cry from the mental images we have perpetuated in our culture.

A point needs to be made here. A servant's heart should not be equated with a milk-toast Christian acquiescence to our culture. At a meeting I heard a man say, "I'll admit I'm a Christian but I feel that pornography is wrong." Admit? Admit what? The poor fellow was defensive and nervous as he halfheartedly attempted to articulate his faith and to apologize for it all in the same sentence.

I don't know which is worse, an anemic halfhearted comment or no comment at all. Somehow I think silence is preferable to a weak-willed, half-believed defense of the biblical world view.

Even though our beliefs might be held by the minority we need not be apologetic. In any event, you don't determine what is true or right by a head count. By the time the man said, "I'll admit I'm a Christian, but . . ." he had already lost the respect of his audience, both Christians and non-Christians alike.

What practically and positively can you do to alter the culture you live in? I suggest you evaluate your own thinking and behaving, making sure you're a part of the solution rather than part of the problem. Begin with the culture of your home, then your church, and then your community. Following are a few ideas to help you evaluate your performance in these three subcultures.

In Your Home

Traditional cultural images of masculinity have treated women as objects to be manipulated, ignored, patronized, or in other ways not taken seriously. Macho men are rarely respected by mentally well-adjusted women. For a man to cling to a macho attitude is both insensitive and immature from a biblical perspective. The Bible indicates that a man should be other-person oriented. We should love and care for our wives as we do ourselves (Eph. 5:28,33).

Peter with the leading of the Spirit of God tells husbands in 1 Peter 3:7-11 that they should give honor to their wives and share everything with them. While no one knows for sure, I think Peter wrote this section of Scripture after he had an argument with his wife. Imagine the following situation: Peter comes home after a hard day working for Jesus. Instead of asking his wife about her day, he says in a demanding way, "When do we eat?" Learning that they will have a nice fish dinner in a few minutes he blurts out with, "What? Fish again?" Or perhaps she wanted to talk with him and he didn't listen. Peter, like many of us, let down at the end of the day and took his wife and family for granted.

Following a hard day with the kids, washing the clothes at the river and cooking the evening meal, Peter's wife wasn't prepared for his insensitivity. She may have left the room in tears. Feeling sorry for himself Peter may have begun to talk to God, "What's wrong with her? I don't understand her sometimes. I try to be a good husband." Peter's prayer doesn't get any higher than his family room ceiling. About this time the Holy Spirit within Peter may have given him verse 7 of 1 Peter 3 which told him, and tells us, that if a husband doesn't live with his wife in an understanding, loving way, his prayers will be virtually worthless. Prayer is never to be used as a substitute for obedience. Realizing his mistake, Peter must have taken the initiative and gone to his wife, comforting her and saying—and meaning—those two difficult words, "I'm sorry." She was gracious and accepted his apology. Only after his reconciliation with his wife was Peter able to again communicate directly with God. Perhaps to summarize the lesson he just learned, Peter says in verse 8, "FInally, all of you, live in harmony with one another; be sympathetic, love as brothers, be compassionate and humble."

Our culture has taught us that historically it is a woman's responsibility to raise the kids. This may be beginning to change. The culture may be responding to the need, as pediatrician Lee Salk claims, "Men have always had a need to be tender and to nurture." Our culture has only recently begun to acknowledge this need, possibly due to the large number of working women. The first significant discussion of the father's role in parenting surfaced following movies such as *Kramer vs. Kramer*. Whatever the recent cultural shifts, the Bible had cited for thousands of years the important role fathers should occupy with their children. As is also true for women, men have the responsibility and the privilege to raise children properly and with love (Deut. 6:2,5). Macho harshness and insensitivity must be avoided (Col. 3:21). At the same time, concerned, involved discipline must be exercised (Eph. 6:4).

Of course an American man doesn't have to be either a husband or father to exercise biblical masculinity. Dr. Gary Collins reminds us that Jesus never married and, possibly, neither did Paul, yet both were exemplary masculine personalities.

Married or not, parent or not, the biblically masculine man treats women and children the same way he treats men—with love and respect.

In the Church

I asked the members of my adult elective Sunday School class what they as individuals could do to befriend both new attenders and established members of our church. The comments were interesting: "Welcome the new people with a smile and a handshake"; "Be hospitable"; "Invite new people to your home for lunch following the service"; "The important thing is not to be pushy but to be available." All agreed that it shouldn't matter what the race, educational level, or income a new person or family had; we should treat them all alike.

With established church people, a class member said,

"We should be available in time of need, not overbearing but there if needed." Another man, a deacon, said, "We should be sensitive to people who are lonely or experiencing some fellowship need."

This is all fine in theory, but our churches, like other institutions, are affected by the impersonality of our culture. Some cult experts agree that many young people turn to cults and way-out sects because they provide at least the appearance of emotional support and love which is lacking in many of our evangelical churches.

Following their conversions to Christ, Henry and Marion Jacobsen said of their effort to find a Bible-believing church that it was difficult to find "the total acceptance and genuine fellowship (which) we took for granted among the Mormons."[26]

Often our principal contact in a new church is with an official greeter, dutifully commissioned and recognizable by his carnation or ribbon. It is his assigned official duty to be nice. The non-greeters sit with their own group and rarely venture forth to meet new people. In one evangelical church a friend of mine attended for several weeks, visitors were told to meet at a certain table for coffee and fellowship following the service. He and his wife took up the challenge and even tried to look as new as possible as they congregated at the visitors' table. Despite their best efforts, after several weeks this gregarious young couple were not made to feel welcome. They left this church and continued their search for a friendly church family.

Our churches copy our culture's corporate model of efficient impersonality. We emphasize structure and organization which often lacks spontaneity and love for one another—not so with the early church. Several years ago David Mains wrote a book, *Full Circle*. He argued that rather than try to get new people to fit into the existing church structure we should alter the structure to allow people the opportunity to express in ministry the gifts given to them by God. Pastor Mains was saying that the church needs to be more human, more interested in people. Larry Richards, commenting about a research project dealing with those whom evangelicals turn to in time of need, said that when personal crisis strikes we're more likely to turn to volunteer community organizations than to a pastor or church friends.[27]

Most of us are instinctively defensive when we are faced with any type of criticism of our church. But we need to realize that this impersonality of our culture has infiltrated our churches. We only pay lip service to Christian values, but in reality we conform to cultural norms more than we should and perhaps more than we realize.

It need not be this way. You can be distinguishable from those who are fully immersed in American culture. As with other areas of your life, you'll need to make a conscious effort to change. Change in small ways at first—smile, say hello, initiate a short conversation, ask fellow parishioners about themselves, be an unofficial greeter. Your greeter status will be recognized because of your inward thoughtfulness, not because of an external ribbon or carnation.

For certain people and occasions you'll need to make a phone call, pay a visit, or write a letter of encouragement. Encourage small *koinonia* groups within the church where individuals can get to know one another better in a spiritual and social environment. Don't always sit with your group during church functions, but rather reach out to others. Encourage lay-person participation in the different responsibilities of the ministries of the local church.

Invite single persons and families to your home for fellowship. A large meal is not necessary to exercise the gift of hospitality. If someone is in need, don't say, "Call me if you need help." No one will call. Rather, say, "I'll bring dinner Monday night" or "I'll drive you to the hospital" or "I'll be over Saturday morning to help in any way I can."

To be transformed in our relationships (Rom. 12:2) requires that we treat people as whole persons—holistically. From witnessing to strangers to helping a friend in need we are required to see people as total beings—people with fears, hurts, grudges, loves, intellect, etc. People play many roles other than just church attenders. People are employees, parents, marriage partners, citizens, taxpayers, learners, etc.

Like our larger culture, the churches have lapsed into a spectator society. In society we passively watch sports instead of playing ourselves. We listen to the Osmonds instead of getting the family around the piano and singing ourselves. We listen too often to the multitudes of so-called experts instead of thinking ourselves, seeking the wisdom and counsel of friends and using the brains God gave us.

The church of all places should be culturally transformed. We should be different. We should be a family of brothers and sisters who care for each other. We are told we will be known by our love for one another (John 13:34,35).

As in a modern family, members of a church family should lighten the load of fellow believers when their individual burdens become extensive (Gal. 6:2). Amish groups take this verse literally. For example, if a man loses his barn to fire or a tornado, his friends and fellow church members, without being asked, get together and work until a new barn is constructed. Breaks are taken during construction to eat food prepared at the work site by the wives. Due to this kind of commitment to each other, Amish tend to feel that insurance, such as social security, is unnecessary. In practical ways we too are to help those in need (Jas. 2:14-17).

Don't confuse culture and life-style with true Christian piety. We often become offended when someone doesn't conform or comply with our cultural brand of Christianity. My wife and I were both church youth leaders during the late 1960s and early 1970s. As you recall, this was a period of social upheaval, which included the Jesus Movement. Well, our college-age youth group sponsored many activities, socials, and home Bible studies in an effort to reach out to unchurched young people. Our group successfully reached many with the gospel of Jesus Christ. Several began to attend the regular services of the church and to grow in their new faith.

One would think the church leaders would be pleased with this outreach. On the contrary. Many of these new and young Christians did not conform to accepted conservative clothing styles. And many had long hair which really irritated the deacon board. In fact, I was called before the church and required to answer questions about why I was encouraging these "long-haired communists" to worship in our church.

I tried to explain that they were not communists, and while I personally didn't care much for long hair on males it seemed a minor point. We should be tolerant and accepting of others, I argued. Besides, isn't it more important what goes on inside of one's head rather than how long hair grows on the outside? Anyhow, many Christians throughout history had long hair. I even showed them a picture of the great English preacher Charles Spurgeon. He was sporting long hair and a full beard.

It was no use. The majority of the deacons had fallen prey to the notion that their brand of conservative American culture, in this case fashion, was somehow Christian. The witness of that church suffered because it majored on what was minor or even irrelevant and had little time left over for caring, loving, and accepting those who might be different. Some of the established church members also seemed to resent that these long-haired people really tried to live as Jesus taught.

Do you need to gain victory over this or some other kind of cultural trap that prevents you from reaching out to others? Reading good books can help. Catherine Marshall tells us in *Something More* that we must release others from our judgment. In the process we release ourselves to be free to love others whom God leads into our lives. We are admonished to put aside cultural distractions and to accept one another (Rom. 15:7) just as Christ has accepted us. Pastor Jerry Cook, in his book *Love, Acceptance and Forgiveness*, shares from his heart how a church can truly reach out to others without being adversely affected by cultural differences. We should not judge. We should rather show practical love to others.

We need to better see what God wants of us without being hindered by viewing through a dark, cultural looking glass. *Christianity Confronts Culture* by Marvin Mayers, while written for missionaries, is useful in helping any Christian "see" his culture more objectively.

In recent years evangelicals are beginning to recognize that the church, like other institutions, can be adversely affected by culture. This is a good trend. In 1982 Lloyd Perry and Norman Shawchuck wrote a book entitled *Revitalizing the Twentieth-Century Church*. These and other authors realize that the church has experienced interpersonal problems and cultural contamination, but now with prayer and God's help, the future will be better.

In Our Community and Country

For too long evangelicals have been uneasy with expressing their ideas in social settings other than church. This is due partially because of feeling inferior, wanting to be liked, and partially because of not wishing to offend another person. But it's OK to share your ideas. Indeed it is essential. In fact it's OK to confront other ideas that are wrong from a biblical perspective. Caution: Confront the issue, not the person. Unless you can have a healthy exchange of ideas with someone, you don't experience interpersonal communication at its best. At its best a relationship needs honest confronting and real caring. You need both.

In an excellent book, *Caring Enough to Confront*, David Augsburger lists how to care and confront at the same time.

Caring	Confronting
I care about our relationship.	I feel deeply about the issue at stake.
I want to hear your view.	I want to clearly express mine.
I want to respect your insights.	I want respect for mine.
I trust you to be able to handle my honest feelings.	I want you to trust me with yours.
I promise to stay with the discussion until we've reached an understanding.	I want you to keep working with me until we've reached a new understanding.
I will not trick, pressure, manipulate, or distort the differences.	I want your unpressured, clear, honest view of our differences.
I give you my loving, honest respect.	I want your caring-confronting response.[28]

Dr. Augsburger is right on the mark. I have a distant relative who is a Christian. This person refuses to discuss any and every topic on which we might possibly hold differing views; this will keep our relationship pleasant and be pleasing to God. But the fact is we really don't have a relationship. We exchange pleasantries, pass on plastic smiles, and that's it. How much better to both care and share as Augsburger suggests.

Robert Lewis Stevenson once said to travel hopefully is better than to arrive. We must realize that our world is not and will not be perfect until Christ returns to this planet. Stan Mooneyham, former president of World Vision, recalled that John Bunyan did not title his book *Pilgrim's Destination* but rather *Pilgrim's Progress*. We have not arrived. We should not be discouraged but rather should work to improve the lives of individuals and the social institutions that so greatly influence all of us.

We must have hope if we are to influence our culture and nation. Don't give up on America or its people. Too many evangelicals have given up mentally, deciding to sit in a mental rocking chair and wait for the Second Coming. The parable of the savorless salt may apply to many of us today.

Our nation is suffering from a decline in absolute biblical values similar to the period of Jewish history when "every man did that which was right in his own eyes" (Judg. 21:25, *KJV*). The result for America could be moral decline, injustice, and political chaos. Without a moral foundation a nation usually degenerates into a state of anarchy. Humans cannot long endure chaos where everyone does his own thing. The absence of a national structure of absolute values ultimately leads to revolution and dictatorship. This pattern has been repeated over and over again in world history. This process is examined in the definitive study by Crane Briton's

Anatomy of Revolution. Writing several decades ago, theologian J. Gresham Machen said you can remove the engineer from a train and witness little initial impact. The train may coast for several miles before stopping. In America, with a crisis of leadership and morality, we may coast for several years. Eventually, however, a day of reckoning will occur.

If *Time* magazine is correct, that some 40 million people claim to be born again in America, we should be having a significant impact upon this culture. To truly influence the culture for good you need to be a positive nonconformist. Yes, a nonconformist. *The Living Bible* paraphrases Romans 12:2 as follows: "Don't copy the behavior and customs of this world, but be a new and different person with a fresh newness in all you do and think." We can influence our culture, especially in a free society based upon a democratic form of government.

The writer in 2 Chronicles 7:14 records the Lord's conditions for cultural and spiritual change: "If my people, who are called by my name, will humble themselves and pray and seek my face and turn from their wicked ways, then I will hear from heaven and will forgive their sin and will heal their land."

Some Christians are beginning to realize that one person's influence can impact the social world of the late twentieth century. Indeed with the Moral Majority we are witnessing a return of fundamentalists to an active involvement in public life. *Listen America*, authored by Jerry Falwell, is the manifesto for this movement. For decades, other more liberal Christians such as Dr. David Moberg in *The Great Reversal: Evangelism Versus Social Concern*, and U.S. Senator Mark Hatfield in *Conflict and Conscience* have argued for evangelical participation in public life for the purpose of changing individual lives as well as social institutions. Francis Schaeffer, in books such as *How Shall We Then Live?* and *Whatever Happened to the Human Race?*, has argued for evangelical involvement in the social order.

Evangelicals hold different views on the issues that confront us and how to solve our nagging and perplexing social problems. But our oneness in Christ, our dependence upon Scripture, prayer, and the direction of the Holy Spirit unite us, make us one in Christ as we individually and collectively influence this great nation.

We may as evangelicals disagree on issues such as E.R.A., defense policy, capitalism, welfare, secular humanism, and other topics, but we can all agree to be caring, concerned, biblically masculine men who reach out to people in need. As with the Samaritan, when we are befriending others, we are not taking time from our lives but are living our lives to the fullest (John 10:10).

Discussion Questions

1. Moses rejected Egypt's life-style. What aspects of America's culture should we reject?

2. If *Time* magazine is correct that there are approximately 40 million born-again Americans, why are we as evangelicals not having more of an impact upon the American culture?

3. How do Christ's masculine traits as listed by Dr. Collins differ from your own? What ideas do you have to help you conform to Christ's example?

4. List some positive ways we can change our culture by exerting a biblical masculinity.

5. How can we better learn to distinguish cultural beliefs from Christian faith?

Chapter 10

How Can a Woman Help?

"A still point in a turning world." *T.S. Eliot*

The message here is mainly for your wife, or perhaps your sister, girl friend or mother. I suggest that you share this chapter with the important woman in your life and solicit her support as you work to enhance the quality of your relationships with other men. End of introduction. Now on to the chapter.

Women Can Help

You might well challenge the basic premise of this book and ask, "Why does my husband need anyone other than me?" Although you agree that friendlessness is not good for one's mental health you may wonder if he really needs anyone else. Perhaps you have followed the magazine articles and books that offer advice on how to keep him happy—massage his ego, say only what he wants to hear, pretend to be what he wants you to be, indulge his every whim. In seminars and books exemplified by Marabel Morgan's *The Total Woman*, women are told to always submit to the president of the family—the man. You are told to revere and even worship him by following the four A's: accept, admire, adopt and appreciate.

These expressed generalizations and oversimplifications sound good and, indeed, contain a measure of truth, but they often break down in the real world of complex problems. When a woman is unable, despite efforts and good intentions, to measure up to the super-woman syndrome, guilt often sets in.

Counselors will quickly tell you that a marriage partner cannot meet all one's needs. A marriage is more healthy when both spouses lead integrated lives. In cases where you find a man who says, "My wife is the only true friend I can turn to," you will also find a wife who says, "I only wish he'd find a friend." A wife cannot meet all the emotional needs of her husband, nor can he meet all of hers.

As a man I tend to want to fight this idea. I want to think I can meet all the needs my wife might have. Grudgingly, however, I must admit that I cannot be all things to even one person. While I believe strongly that husband and wife should be the closest of friends, and the marriage relationship is more important than a friendship, there is room for and a need for same-sex friendships. However, friendships outside marriage, while important, must not detrimentally interfere with family activities. A husband and wife's principal responsibility in human relationships is to each other and to their children. You must protect your family's time together and not allow a friendship to steal inordinate amounts of time from the family. Close friendships established on the biblical model realize the importance of the marriage and family relationship, and therefore do not allow the friendship to compete with family responsibilities.

But the fact remains that your husband needs friends, and if the relationships are biblical they will enhance rather than detract from the marriage relationship. Your husband needs quality friendships to add balance and sharing to his way of living.

How can you help the man in your life develop close interpersonal relationships? Answers to this question which I asked in questionnaires, include the following:

"Encourage him to see his friends in our home; allow him time."

"Encourage him to reach out, to be more personal, to do things with other men."

"Create an atmosphere in which he is free to grow as a person."

"Let him know it's not a crime to let his feelings show."

"I need to point out his good qualities. I need to draw him out more, to get him to express his feelings."

Almost without exception these women believe it is important to encourage their men to develop male friendships. And *encourage* is the theme of this chapter, for it is through an active encouragement that you will be able to help your husband with his interpersonal relationships.

In earlier chapters we discussed how the rigidity of the macho male prevents growth of relationships of closeness of any quality. Psychotherapist Edward B. Fish is of the opinion that macho men would disappear like snowballs in July if women stopped making it so heavenly for them. Therefore, to help a man help himself may mean going against the grain to some extent. You may need to expand, go beyond the traditional and narrow definition of what a woman's role consists of in a man's life.

You can help your husband by helping him prioritize his activities and thinking to coincide with biblical values. Jerry and Mary White in their book *The Christian in Mid-Life* report that all too often a man awakens too late and discovers that his family and friends have lived for years in the shadow of his work and ambition. A wife should encourage her husband to lead a more enjoyable, balanced life which includes—in moderation—each of the following: work, play, church, community service, family, and friends.

Establish a Balance

Norm Wright believes that "the more a man centers his identity in just one phase of his life—such as vocation, family, or career—the more vulnerable he is to threats against his identity and the more prone he is to experience a crisis. A man who has limited sources of identity is potentially the most fragile. Men . . . need to broaden their basis for identity. They need to see themselves in several roles rather than *just* a teacher, *just* a salesman, *just* a handsome, strong male, *just* a husband."[29]

Help your husband to recognize and experience his different selves. If your husband tends to become overly intellectual during almost any discussion you may want to draw him out emotionally by asking how he feels about the topic at hand. Give him the freedom to express his inner feelings. Make sure you don't reject his feelings once you begin to hear them, however. It's OK to be silly and moonstruck—listening together to an "oldie but goodie" tune and then a moment later, seeing life passing by, to launch into an intellectual or spiritual discussion about life's meaning. Different moods and emotions complement our lives.

Encourage your husband to be a well-rounded human being. Too many people have a "me first" mind-set. Many sad people are too concerned with themselves, their jobs or with "finding themselves" rather than with their families and friends. Some men and women talk about an identity crisis—"I don't know who I am." These people fail to grasp the biblical principle that identity comes not from selfishness but from concern and relationships with other people.

It's currently fashionable to twist relationships that traditionally require commitment—such as to parents, marriage partner, children and friends—until we are free to be ourselves (whatever that means) no matter what the costs. The end of this selfishness is usually frustration and sadness.

This inordinate concern with self is unheard of in most other cultures, where the family, friends, and even the community come before the individual. Christian women need to build the confidence of their husbands and to encourage their development as well-rounded human beings. To do this requires that their husbands commit themselves to another, which is a form of self-denial. This, of course, cuts both ways but men especially need the mature love and devotion only their wives can give. I'm convinced that there is nothing more important to a man than to know that his wife truly cares for him. And conversely, a man is quickly devastated by a wife's insensitive criticism. We as men are a vulnerable breed.

In my own life I firmly believe that my gregarious nature is largely the result of the rich, supportive relationship I enjoy with my wife, Sue Ann. Without her love and genuine concern for my welfare, I'm sure I'd be a very different person. Maybe it's the little boy that remains in all men, i.e., we need to constantly have the support of the women we love. Sue Ann not only tells me she loves me, she gives specific reasons for her love. This is one of the greatest things a wife can do for her spouse.

While I was conducting research for this book, one 45-year-old man I interviewed told me, "I work with men under stressful situations. These guys don't know how to express emotions. My wife has taught me to bring my feelings out. I'm a better man today because of her. She really cares about me." Without this support on the home front a man is less likely to be outgoing and concerned about others. Support on the home front helps a man develop his identity to his full potential.

Don't Expect Too Much

In many ways many men, despite the accumulation of chronological adult status, remain little boys at heart. Dr. Theodore I. Rubin, monthly columnist for *Ladies Home Journal*, has said on several occasions that the American society tends to produce mature women but for some reason most men remain little boys with traits such as abnormal insecurity, frustration, jealousy, insensitivity, apprehension and all the rest. Dr. Rubin believes that women need to know that many men:

● Retain more of the "little boy" than women do the "little girl"

● Don't like to admit they are dependent

● Are fearful, jealous, and contemptuous of women

● Will not admit to soft, warm feelings which they consider feminine

● Feel they must be strong, i.e., stubborn, competitive, etc.

● Are unable to establish mature men-to-men friendships because of a fear of homosexuality

● Have difficulty relating to children because of their own childlike characteristics—they see their own children as competitors for their wife's affection, time and energy

● Are unable to measure up to masculine ideals, are prone to self-depreciation

- Won't admit it but they crave affection; men want to be coddled and fussed over, especially in stressful times
- Are vulnerable to vanity and are concerned with being young-looking and sexually appealing
- Measure self-esteem in terms of power and money
- Fear loneliness even more than women; many men are afraid of leisure time and vacations and do not adjust well to retirement since most of their psychological support is derived from work
- Are frightened by the possibility of rejection by women.[30]

Men are different to be sure, and perhaps a little strange too. It is men more than women who are unpredictable, illogical, and often downright crazy. I hope you'll allow your husband a little madness in harmless areas. Don't require an explanation for everything. The poor fellow won't always be able to provide one for all of his behavior.

Work at seeing his world through his eyes. Be realistic. In your effort to help him help himself, don't expect miracles. Dr. Amitai Etzioni and most other social scientists are of the opinion that human behavior is difficult to change. This is true for either productive or negative behavior. Don't expect too much. Dr. Theodore Rubin observes that women tend to idealize men. Idealization does not leave room for human limitations, and when the man turns out to have faults or is unwilling or unable to fit the image, disappointment follows.

We often expect too much of men. Psychologist Herb Goldberg says that society has placed confusing expectations on the married male, demanding that he be all things to all people: the capable provider, the aggressive competitor, the wise father, the sensitive and gentle lover, the fearless protector, the controlled one under pressure, and the emotionally-expressive person at home.

As a wife, do you add to the pressure of your husband or do you ease his burdens? Are you satisfied with what he provides or do you leave the impression that you need a larger home and he is always one raise behind?

Men change slowly in their relationships if they change at all. Billy Graham says he is amazed by men who spend days successfully analyzing a problem in their business and yet seem unwilling or incapable of analyzing what is wrong with either their marriage or friendships.

It's easy to criticize men for their general lack of nurturing relationships. To be helpful, however, a woman needs to accept him as he is, and this includes minimizing his weaknesses and building on his strengths. Be tolerant and understanding if his friendship skills evolve slowly. Remember, other men have trouble with this too, adding to your husband's difficulty. Remember also that your husband spends his days with men he must compete with or who are either of a higher or lower status. Therefore, the work place is not always the best environment for men to develop friendships.

When your husband does begin to cultivate friendships, don't criticize them. Donna, a woman about 39 or 40, told me that criticism is deadly to a marriage relationship. This is especially true if it's done in the presence of relatives, neighbors, or friends, or as gossip behind his back. If you must criticize, schedule a time for the two of you to talk, but never speak negatively of him or his friends to others. This is deadly to the male ego. Donna said, "It is I who creates the emotional tone of our home. I respect his friends and try to take at least some interest in them."

In 1937, Dale Carnegie wrote a book that sold eight million copies because his advice was so practical. Some may argue that his *How to Win Friends and Influence*

People is dated or even corny, but I disagree. His ideas are useful and for the most part, founded on biblical principles.

Dale Carnegie gives several principles for building friendships. The following ideas are adapted from Carnegie's book. If you apply these basic ideas in your marriage relationship your husband will be more able to cultivate man-to-man friendships. According to Carnegie the best way to make more and lasting friendships is to get your mind off yourself and to take a genuine interest in other people. Be generous and sincere with praise when you see positive changes. Don't be critical of another's behavior. It only makes him defensive. Rather get people to express their ideas and listen to and be respectful of their ideas even if you don't fully agree with what's being said.[31]

Good advice for everyone, men and women alike. We need to value and give our attention to the development of the internal things of the heart and spirit. The point of 1 Peter 3:1-6, for example, is that jewelry, clothes, cosmetics and other externals are not very important despite what we hear daily from newspaper, radio, and TV ads. A primary emphasis on these external things will do little to either build a good marriage or help your husband form quality friendships.

Be a Positive Role Model

Before you can help a man develop friendships, your own relationship with him must be good. You must be a trusted confidante, one he feels free to turn to in time of need. And even then don't expect someone to change directly because of your advice, no matter how good you know it to be. Remember your influence upon others results only indirectly. So if you want someone else to change, look first at your own behavior.

Talk is cheap. People can be won over without a word due to one's manner of life. In fact, a man can hardly be changed in any other fashion.

Women can be assertive in a thoughtful and gentle way which may lead a husband to a changed life. This occurred dramatically in my own life. Typically, I followed the crowd during my teen years. I had no real plans or goals of my own. Frequently I found myself in trouble in school, causing my mother grief. My father had died when I was 12.

After three semesters I found little that interested me, so I dropped out of college. My life-style didn't bother me. It never occurred to me that I might be missing out on something—until I met Sue Ann in 1963.

It didn't take long for me to see that she had something different. I was particularly impressed with her family. And I saw an assurance in Sue Ann's life. She really seemed to have everything together.

One afternoon, she told me what made her life special. Jesus Christ. She said being a Christian was a matter of faith. I could do nothing good enough to earn my way into heaven. No one could. But Christ had already taken the punishment for my sins by dying on the cross. Somehow everything she told me made sense.

Our discussion was purely intellectual, but it started getting to me. Later when I was alone I realized I needed God in my life. I prayed that God would forgive my sins, and I received Christ as my Saviour.

My life was changed. God gave me contentment in place of restlessness. He gave me purpose in place of aimlessness. He exchanged my apathy for a thirst for knowledge. In the words of C.S. Lewis, "I was surprised by joy." God really did change me.

Several months later Sue Ann and I were married. Why did I respond to her sharing with me from Scripture?

It wasn't her words; it was the way she lived her life. The way she lived led me to want to hear her words.

Major on the Majors

Don't be distracted. Stay on track.

Perhaps you recall the time when Christ, on His journey to Jerusalem, stopped off at the home of Martha and Mary. The Lord needed human fellowship as He contemplated the agony of His anticipated suffering and death.

Mary listened to Jesus as He spoke. But "Martha was distracted by all the preparations that had to be made." And Martha apparently resented her sister's seeming idleness. Martha said, "Lord, don't you care that my sister has left me to do the work by myself?" Jesus responded directly, "Mary has chosen what is better" (Luke 10:38-42).

Martha's concern with the meal is not wrong in itself. We all have to eat. Both sisters loved Jesus and were doing what they thought best at the moment. But timing and priorities must be considered. D.L. Moody's observation was that the good is often the enemy of the best. This was true for Martha during the Lord's visit. You must guard against and be aware of the bareness of a busy life. Women are particularly susceptible to this danger because of the endless tasks that must be accomplished on the domestic front. Set lesser matters aside frequently and concentrate upon developing and nurturing an in-depth relationship with your husband. Don't neglect that which you know to be important.

Read together. Share ideas together. Listen to each other. Take a long drive and talk about anything and everything. Schedule a break in the routine. Have breakfast together. Walk or exercise together. Plan to spend some time together each day without distractions. You decide what to do together but make a conscious choice to do things that are important.

Don't neglect the important relationships you and your husband share.

Plan for the Future

Kids make friends easily. Children seek personal bonds because of a need for love. Only later do they learn to artificially suppress these needs. Parents teach their kids, especially boys, to stop being so outgoing. So in addition to helping your husband you can begin also to impact upon the next generation. The hand that rocks the cradle will change the world. The way you rear a child now will directly influence his adult life.

This is true for all cultures. For example, Dr. Margaret Mead, in her book *Sex and Temperament in Three Primitive Societies*, pointed out that a strong association exists between child-rearing practices and later personality development. Children who received a good deal of attention and gentleness, as among the New Guinea mountain Arapesh, became cooperative, unaggressive, friendly adults. But children of the New Guinea Mundugomor community, who were raised with perfunctory and intermittent attention, developed into uncooperative, aggressive and unfriendly adults. The Bible records in Proverbs 22:6, "Train a child in the way he should go, and when he is old he will not turn from it."

What you do to and for children will have lasting influence. How do you treat your sons differently from your daughters? Do you make sweeping statements that lead your children to think of gender rather than individuals? Do you discourage your son from expressing his true feelings and emotions with a "boys don't cry" comment? Dr. Joyce Brothers suggests that you make sure your son and daughter rotate tasks such as dishes, gardening, lawn mowing, etc., so that these jobs are not sex oriented. Also think before you buy toys. What impact will they have on the child? What are your kids reading at school and for leisure? Does the material reinforce distorted macho images of what is manly?

Helping Kids Make Friends is a book about how to help children develop friendship skills. Making friends can be taught. The authors advise:

- Provide many opportunities for children to interact with other kids at a very young age.

- Provide games and activities that involve children in cooperative types of play, such as painting a mural, instead of individual activities.

- Teach children to accept no for an answer and to realize we don't always get what we want.

- Provide plenty of models for children to learn what it means to share. For example while watching a TV show encourage them to notice what the good guy does to be likeable when he relates to others.

- There are lots of children's books in libraries and bookstores about friendships, making friends, moving to a new neighborhood or losing friends. All are helpful tools in getting to talk with your child about making friends.

- If you point out other children to your child who behave well, do it in a subtle way that does not demean your youngster. For example, saying, "Look how much Sarah likes it when Johnny shares the model airplane with her," is much more effective than, "Look how nice Johnny is; why can't you be like that?"

- We criticize our children too often. Try to notice the good things they are doing and build on that. Follow up with justified praise.

- If the parents have an easy time making friends, so will the children. Let your kids learn from your example.[32]

An important method of helping both son and father

develop skills of relationship building is to encourage your husband to take more of the child-rearing responsibilities in your family. By spending more time with his children a man will acquire an ability to express his emotions more fully, and the sons along with daughters will learn that it's OK for a dad to parent his children.

Discussion Questions

1. How can you change another person's behavior indirectly?

2. Develop a daily plan to provide your spouse with support and encouragement. List the specifics of such a plan.

3. In what ways, like Martha in Luke 10, are you distracted from developing better communication skills?

4. Using God's promise in Proverbs 22:6, discuss the extent of our influence and responsibility as parents in helping sons to develop wholesome friendships.

Chapter 11

Developing New Friendships

"A man must get friends as he would get food and drink for nourishment and sustenance." *Randolph S. Bourne*

If you have few or perhaps no close friendships, you need to change both your thinking and behavior. Why should you change? You really don't have a choice. No one plans to live a mediocre, friendless life. To do otherwise requires a conscious effort to change the way you think and act. A deliberate effort is needed to locate, establish, and maintain friendships.

You may be a man who blames your wife, parents, childhood or some other personal background force for your current friendless condition. Men can find professional psychologists, many with Freudian or Skinnerian backgrounds, who will agree with them on this. But it's of little comfort if you're going through life without experiencing the joys which come from intimate friendships.

You can change. Begin by taking conscious control over your present situation. Ask God to give you the strength of purpose to alter those aspects of your personality that block or prevent the development of close relationships. Don't worry about yesterday or the many yesterdays. You can't do anything about your past anyway. It's recorded history.

Dr. William Glasser has introduced a new movement within psychology which many feel is more useful than the earlier ideas of Freud and Jung. Glasser in his *Reality Therapy*, rather than lamenting that we are helpless victims of our past, tells us that we have the power to overcome our past. Deal with today; it's all you can work with anyway. Perhaps you've seen the poster that reads, "Today is the first day of the rest of your life." Well, it's true, and only you and God can take control of your life if changes are required. Old things can pass away and new things can occur (2 Cor. 5:17).

How can you change? Admittedly it's difficult to change the way you feel and act. This is especially true if you have been wounded emotionally. Once we are hurt, few of us want to risk being vulnerable again. But change is possible if you follow two courses of action: First, change your behavior by putting into practice both the biblical principles of chapter 4 and the personality traits discussed in chapter 5. The following pages will also provide a few examples to help stimulate you to begin the process of change in small, manageable, realistic ways. Second, follow the course of action discussed in the last part of this chapter—broaden the number and kinds of men who qualify as potential friends.

Norman Vincent Peale tells the story of a terribly upset vice-president of a company who had just been passed over for the president's position. A new man had been brought in from the outside. The vice-president was riled. But the new president needed the support, friendship and love of the vice-president.

Rev. Peale told him that tough as it might be, "I would swallow my disappointment, forget my wounded ego, walk into that man's office and tell him I wanted to help him all I could. You see, that new executive is lonely. He knows how the organization feels about him and he needs help. Believe me, he needs you. Practice empathy. Put yourself in his shoes and also try the Golden Rule on him. 'Do unto others as you wish they would do unto you.' I think it will pay off all the way around. Love 'em is the answer."

The vice-president buried his pride and applied the suggestion. As a result the two men established an excellent working relationship. Two years later the president moved on to a new organization. You guessed it. Before leaving he recommended that the vice-president succeed him. The new president now has a framed legend on the wall which reads, "Love 'Em."[33] I'm sure Rev. Peale would agree that the important thing is not that a president's position was won but rather that the two men learned to depend upon each other and developed a warm, working relationship.

Sadly this kind of relationship rarely exists in the business community where men learn early to look out for number one as they fight their way up the professional ladder.

A few years ago sociologists from Duke University interviewed hundreds of people to find out why some were happy and others unhappy. They discovered that those who are happy live in the present and future but not the past. The Duke study also found that happy people do not waste time and energy fighting conditions that cannot be changed.

Contented people, instead of complaining about not having friends, seek to enter into the lives of others. I've mentioned before, when you involve yourself in someone's life you take risks, you're vulnerable, or at least you feel vulnerable. This risk taking is even evident with the seemingly minor things in life such as letter writing. As the following story indicates, we must take the small risks. Take the slight chance that you'll be rejected, because to do otherwise is to miss some of the greatest joys of life.

Early in the history of our republic the sacrifice and wisdom of John Adams and Thomas Jefferson, along with other men and women, helped to establish the new American nation. While they shared a love for the new United States, these two men had lost affection for each other. Some historians feel that the arrogance and abrasive personality of John Adams caused a falling-out with many of his contemporaries, not just with Jefferson. This political and personal hostility was very noticeable when, following Jefferson's election in 1800, Adams even refused to attend the new President's inauguration.

Years passed. There was a complete lack of communication between these two statesmen. Long after Jefferson's two-term presidency, when Jefferson was 68 and Adams was 76, a brief letter from Adams arrived at Monticello, Virginia. Adams simply stated that he and his family were well and enclosed specimens of homespun yarn. It wasn't the content but rather the signature that gladdened the heart of Thomas Jefferson. The letter was signed, "With sincere esteem, your friend and servant— John Adams." This simple letter initiated a classic correspondence in American history.

In his excellent biography of Jefferson, Saul Padover says that "time had blunted the sharp edges of their political differences, and now that both were in retirement they could resume a friendship that was started way back when they were both comparatively young rebels against the crown."

Actually it was the concern of Dr. Benjamin Rush,

also a signer of the Declaration of Independence, who admired both men, that brought the two together. Of the correspondence which followed, Saul Padover says, "The two old gentlemen, both men of massive learning and vase intellectual curiosity, poured out their ideas with the zeal and zest of youngsters. To the intimacy of their letters they entrusted their innermost hopes and fears and prejudices and convictions and indignations."[34] And it must be remembered that without the concerned intervention of Dr. Rush, both Adams and Jefferson would have missed the joy that resulted from this noble relationship.

Before moving to Indiana last year my wife and I met monthly with three other couples from our church for fellowship and Bible study. Our times together were refreshing spiritually and socially. We remember well the good conversations, laughter, and on occasion the sharing of personal concerns. A few months before we packed our bags, one of these families moved to the East Coast. We missed them and felt a sense of personal loss.

As I was preparing to write this book I went through all of my files looking for relevant material on the subject of male relationships. In one folder I discovered a letter I had written to the friend who moved to Massachusetts. In my letter I mentioned that we missed him and Jane, and that I was looking for a new job; I wrote that Sue Ann had found a challenging women's Bible study and that the kids were doing well in school. I asked my friend David if he liked his new graduate level teaching position. I cited a few other insignificant facts and closed with "give our love to Jane and the children." I signed the letter and then almost defensively added, "P.S.—this is National Letter Writing Week. Men seem to need excuses to write."

What I have to admit is that the letter in my file was

the original copy. I didn't send the letter. It may be hard to believe, but even though the letter was written, I didn't mail it. I didn't know at the time why I put the letter in my files rather than in the mail. It's very difficult for each of us to understand our own emotions and the reasons behind our individual behavior.

I have an idea, however, why David never received my letter. To begin with, I didn't believe the letter was very intellectual. The intended receiver of the letter is a few years older than I and is very intelligent. I guess I didn't want to seem dumb or silly to this urbane gentleman whom I respect. Also, I didn't have much of anything to say and therefore had no reason to write. But when you boil it down, one salient reason for not sending the letter emerges: after all, I wouldn't want him to feel obligated to answer. We were not all that close and he might think it odd that I was attempting to start up a correspondence. I was afraid that I would be rejected. You see, I couldn't predict with any degree of accuracy how he might react to my letter, so I refused to risk possible rejection.

A few months later, when Sue Ann and I were agonizing over a possible move and the accompanying change in jobs, she encouraged me to call David since he had recently struggled with a similar job change experience. I put it off. She persisted. When I finally did call, our conversation was quite enjoyable and he gave me some ideas which helped my family deal with the new job offer. But more important, the call helped to maintain a friendship. While the analogy may be stretched somewhat, Sue Ann's encouragement was for me what Dr. Rush had been for Adams and Jefferson.

The lesson to be learned is this: take the time and the risk with small things. This is how friendships begin. Letters, smiles, luncheons, sharing, questions, listening, helping, and countless other small activities are building blocks to friendship.

Soon after arriving in my new position as curriculum director for a suburban Indianapolis school corporation, I received two letters from friends with whom I used to work. I was thrilled to get both letters. John's letter began: "Hope you are settled in with your family and have not started too many new curriculum projects yet." He continued, "An old Jesuit once told me to distrust any man who wants to change something before he knows what it is." I appreciated my friend John's thoughtful advice.

The other letter also produced a smile as old memories were recalled and new information shared. This letter closed with the words, "I miss you, David." I appreciated so much this man's willingness to open up and share with me the fact that I am important to him. These few words had an impact on me. He lifted my spirits with his acknowledgment of our friendship and his feelings.

Little things really are important aren't they? So express your friendly feelings in some small way, like writing a letter that really doesn't have to be written. Or reach out in some other way that you feel comfortable with. You'll feel better and you may reap the rich dividends of closer, more nurturing, interpersonal relationships.

Research reveals that interpersonal relationships are either won or lost in the critical first four minutes of meeting a new individual. Imagine it, we form opinions of others we have just met in a brief and yet vital first four minutes. Our eye contact, our handshake, our first words—the small things—make the crucial impact. In his famous book *How to Win Friends and Influence People* Dale Carnegie lists several practical ways to make people like you. The ideas are not profound but they work. For example we need to learn to smile, to show genuine interest by remembering a man's name, to listen sincerely and to encourage others to talk about themselves and their interests. By making others feel important a climate for creating friendships is established.[35]

Sure, we need to work at it and we shouldn't be self-centered, but the rules of developing a friendship are little more than a series of small things, small steps which lead to satisfying relationships.

In his book on friendship Dr. Harold Dawley provides a summary of the rules of friendship making. Here are his eight points.

Rule 1—*Like yourself.* Think of yourself in positive ways and work toward being a friend to yourself.

Rule 2—*Reach out.* Reach out to people in subtle and direct ways so that you are in a good position for friendships to develop.

Rule 3—*Make contact.* Be accessible to people—both in the physical and psychological sense—since potential friendships surround you awaiting your contact.

Rule 4—*Be pleasant.* Strive to have a pleasing effect on people by being polite, giving genuine compliments, smiling and engaging in similar positive behaviors.

Rule 5—*Get to know people.* Directing your interest to others and away from yourself allows you to get to know the other person.

Rule 6—*Let people know you.* Reveal personal, intimate thoughts and feelings to others at the right time and people will be able to see and understand you as you really are.

Rule 7—*Get through to people.* Effective communication enables you to say exactly what you want so that confusion and misunderstanding are minimized.

Rule 8—*Get along with people.* Handle conflict effectively by seeing the other person's view; letting him talk it out, avoiding resentment while standing up for your legitimate rights, are good ways of getting along with people.[36]

It's the little things like eye contact and other nonverbal signals, asking people questions, and saying thank you at the right time that make or break a relationship. Of the ten lepers healed by Christ, one—only one—wasn't all of a sudden too busy to return to give thanks. Dale Carnegie said, "You can make more friends in two months by becoming interested in other people than you can in two years by trying to get other people interested in you."

A group of divinity students at Princeton failed a "Good Samaritan" test because they were in too much of a hurry. Forty unwitting theology students were asked by researchers to go across campus for a special television taping session. On their way the divinity students encountered a "victim" slumped in a doorway, coughing, groaning, and in apparent pain. Aware of a man in apparent distress, only 16 of the 40 seminarians stopped to help the man. The moral: A man in a hurry is likely to keep going and, in the process, miss opportunities for both service and friendship.

A plaque entitled "A Friend" recently caught my eye. It read, "A friend is one who knows you as you are, understands where you've been, accepts who you've become and still gently invites you to grow." Our attitude about ourselves as well as about others is important. Dr. Clyde Narramore believes that one of the important traits of emotional health is belief in your own likeableness. A second trait of emotional health is the corresponding belief that others are likeable too. These truths were expressed in the best-seller of a few years ago, *I'm OK— You're OK* by Thomas Harris.

We must be aware that the people we meet in life are "OK." Don't neglect the biblical principle that all people are created and loved by God. We must, therefore, view all individuals as important and certainly worthy of our time and attention, and that potential friends can be found anywhere.

Moving is always a tough job. Accumulating all that is needed (or should I say wanted?) to keep a family functioning makes moving day a mixed blessing. Our most recent move from Northbrook, Illinois to Noblesville, Indiana was a case in point. Three different neighbors whom I had helped move to nearby suburbs, learning of my anticipated departure, insisted on returning the favor. So, following two high estimates from professional movers I decided to do it myself. I accepted my previous neighbors' offer to help as well as that from some current neighbors.

The day before we moved, my wife and most—if not all—of the neighborhood women had a gigantic garage sale on our front lawn. It was a happening—buying, selling, and bartering more among each other than from the infrequent bona fide shoppers to our neighborhood flea market. We laughed and cried. Actually, the women let a few tears flow; the men, expressing their emotions a little differently, resorted to hearty handshakes.

Then on our last night in town a couple from our church called to say good-bye. After talking briefly they said, "We're all going out for dinner." As tired as we were it would have been easier to stay at home and open a couple of cans of food. I'm glad we didn't. I'm also glad that we assented to our neighbors' offer to help. It's easy to avoid asking or accepting help, often because we can purchase our own things and also others' services. We do it ourselves, thereby cutting off potential close relationships. The result is a self-sufficient form of social isolation.

Not only did we receive help in moving, but during our search for a new home in Indiana we were fortunate to have the help and concern of two businessmen in the city. At first I was impatient with the pleasantries and later grew skeptical of the kindness of these men. I wondered why a business person such as our realtor would invite us to his home for dinner and a neighborhood cookout. When I introduced myself to a vice-president of a local bank, and began immediately to ask about interest rates and other related financial matters, the banker gently interrupted my inquiries with questions about my family, the move, and my new position as curriculum director for the local school corporation. Then he said, "How do you like our town?" I finally slowed down to listen and even share something of myself.

Finally I came to realize that these men, while businessmen to be sure, were also interested in me as a person. Long after we purchased our home I continued to associate with these men. The realtor and the banker may not become lifelong close friends, but then again maybe they will. What's important is that they made an effort to be friendly and I responded. With the hustle and bustle of house and mortgage hunting it would have been easy to handle everything alone, forgetting that potential friends can be found anywhere. This illustrates the simple yet profound truth that "to have friends, be friendly."

Expand Your Standards

Potential friends can indeed be found anywhere if you're willing to be more aware and open to men you have just met as well as those you have known for years. Even when we believe we are willing to form new friendships, usually we limit ourselves to the person who meets our very limited criteria to qualify as a possible friend. Friends tend to be selected from the same social class, race, political party, and age range.

Other factors prejudice our often subconscious views

on who is a possible friend. My father told me shortly before his death that a man's character may be measured by the way he treats people that have little or no impact upon his life. I have tried to remember and practice this principle, but not always successfully.

Like the time a poorly dressed man asked me for 50 cents so he could get some food. I was too busy, or so I believed at the time, to take the man to lunch. And I was unwilling to give him the money he requested, trying to convince myself that if I did give him money, it would soon turn into a shot and a beer anyway.

But what if he really needed the money? I could have at least taken time for a little simple human conversation. All I would have lost would have been a few cents and a few minutes of my time. What I actually lost was the opportunity to involve myself in the life of another person. By keeping my money and my time I became a loser, similar to the priest and Levite who refused to help the traveler on the road outside Jerusalem. We as men need to consciously and prayerfully break out of our limited view of the world. God loves the man who asked me for money as much as He loves me. We need to pray that God will help us view the world and its inhabitants from His perspective.

It's difficult for men to take a sincere interest in others. Our thinking tends to be task oriented not people oriented. We think of jobs to be done rather than individuals who need appreciation and recognition.

A retired milkman worked as a janitor in the high school where I taught for several years. We talked daily. Neither of us let the large difference in age and job roles prevent us from enjoying each other's company. We even asked about each other's families and personal interests.

One day as we were talking we both realized that this

dear man had known my father when they both worked for Borden Dairy. We both laughed as we learned of the connection between us. He enjoyed sharing with someone who would really listen. And it was a thrill for me to discover more about my father, who had died suddenly when I was only 12 years old. It's ironic that the principle my dad taught me of extending kindness to others had helped to bring this retired man and me together.

Another older man (Lee is now 85) befriended me following my father's death in 1955. He gave me the time and attention I needed as an impressionable teenager. I believe he even risked his life when he taught me to drive a car in a remote cemetery when I was 15. And in another incident, I'll never forget his tolerance and kindness when, misjudging the length of a pier, I wrecked the front of his boat. He knew I felt badly about what happened. We're still friends, now nearly 30 years later.

In more recent years I have been able to return a few of his many friendly acts. Lee extended himself to a young boy and in the process made a lifelong friend. At the same time I acquired a father figure who has meant a great deal to me through the years.

I have another friend who is many years my junior. This troubled me at first, but we share a good deal in common as do our wives. As a couple we worked closely together while a church building program was under way and during these past few years have developed what will be a lifelong relationship.

Don't let age get in your way. When you meet a potential friend of a different age don't immediately shut him out of your life.

Much of our socializing in America is done with people almost identical to ourselves. Diversity is sacrificed for a humdrum similarity. Old people are isolated from the young. Rich and poor rarely meet or understand each other. The same is true for politics, religion, race, education, occupation, age, and marital status. It's as if we'll use any excuse to avoid one another.

An old people's home was constructed about a mile from the high school where I was teaching several years ago. Both buildings were off to themselves on the outskirts of town. Unlike other cultures, we in America relegate both the young and old to an unproductive, noninvolved existence. I attempted to bring these two worlds together. Our program was called Y.O.U., Young and Old United. It was beautiful. They learned and helped each other. In our cultures where extended families still exist, people of different ages are able to learn from and contribute to the lives of people of different generations. Perhaps through groups like Y.O.U. or adopt-a-grandparent program we can reclaim an important heritage.

People of varied social or economic backgrounds rarely develop close relationships. This is somewhat understandable since diverse educational and income levels produce people with varied interests. The Bible warns, however, against discriminating against people of different social class, especially the poor. From the Epistle of James, for example, we learn that giving favorite treatment to a man with wealth, while ignoring the poor man, is wrong (2:1-7).

Upon meeting someone for the first time, one of the first questions men ask is, "What do you do?" What we want to know is their occupation, and with it their social standing. We hear the response to our question and then pigeonhole the person as someone to know better or someone not worth spending much time on. We need to break out of the rut of equating the worth of a person with his occupation.

American values have not changed a great deal since Vance Packard wrote *Status Seekers* in the late 1950s.

The belief that what a man does for a living is the best measure of his worth is as false today as it was years ago. A man of great character may have a menial job while someone with high status in his job may be, for example, a failure as a parent or husband.

While conducting research on social class differences for a sociology article, I decided to do some field work. My approach was what sociologists refer to as participant observation. For a few days I arrived at 5:30 A.M. at a day-labor employment agency on the north side of Chicago. I was poorly dressed, and unshaven. At about 6:00 A.M. each day my name was called and I was herded on a bus and driven to a factory that needed extra short-term menial help. The work was tiring. I spent all day on an assembly line packing rat poison. The pay was less than minimum wage.

We were like untouchables. Almost no one would talk to us except to give orders. Even eye contact was rare. It was like we didn't exist. It was an eerie feeling to be ignored. Although I was in the plant for only a few days, I nevertheless had a strong desire to tell people who I really was. Each of us wants to be recognized even by strangers. Since that day-labor experience I've wondered if there were any middle-class Christians in the factory who may have ignored me and others.

What I did discover is that even very poor people are willing to share. A poor man on the day-labor bus offered me conversation and one-half of his sandwich. Other than their poverty, and in some cases broken English, these men I worked and talked with were indistinguishable from men of other social classes.

This is not to suggest that you go out and plan to find people who are different from you. On the contrary, the best friendships are usually between people of related interests and backgrounds. The point I wish to make is simply this: relate to people as individuals not as members of racial, economic, or social groups. Potential friends can be found in unsuspecting places if you are willing to look.

Don't limit your friendships to popular and very likeable individuals. Rather look among ordinary people for men with great character. Some of these you may already know but have not taken the time to get to know well.

On an August day in 1977 Julius Loh died. Other ordinary Americans died that day, 5478 to be exact. Some years before Mr. Loh's death, his son Jules asked his dad in irreverent jest, "Tell me, Pop, what you've done that you're proud of that no one else has done, because someday I'm going to write your obituary." Mr. Loh responded, "I've turned in three fire alarms, none false."

Writing of his father's death for the *Chicago Sun Times* an older, wiser, sadder son recorded these words. "In his own time, this man survived the Depression, barely, not to mention four wars and other assorted upheavals of three generations and all the while kept both his family and his sense of humor intact.

"If this is an ordinary life, then genius is indeed the apt word. At least one of his children never stopped long enough in his own self-centered life to realize that fact until it was too late to realize, even that his father was mortal, that the old man would not always be there, as ordinary as a mooring post.

"That son, who once asked you what you were proud of, Pop, is, in his sorrow, awfully proud to bear your name." Speaking of his dad, and also for all but a handful of the others that died on that summer day, Jules Loh said, "They were born, lived decently and justly, turning in no false alarms, worked hard, honored their spouses, begat children and saw to their upbringing, minded their business and died without debt."

There are millions of good people in this world, many of whom you work with, live near or who even live within your own family. Reach out to them, really get to know them, discover their physical, emotional and spiritual needs. The result will be warm, meaningful friendships.

What will happen? The love you learn to extend to others will be returned manyfold. Ask for God's help to make you a caring, concerned individual. God's love, working through you, will eliminate much of your shyness and fear.

While preparing this chapter I asked my wife, Sue Ann, what a friendless American man should do to make and keep friends. She gave me a number of good ideas, many of which are included in this book. But one comment seemed to stand out as basic. She said, "Men need to view other men as individuals who have intrinsic worth and dignity as creatures of God. And therefore each person you meet is worth knowing at a personal level."

I asked Sue Ann what is the best way for men to follow through on this truth that each man is worth knowing at an in-depth level. She said, "First, a man must look for a need so that he can offer help." The Apostle Paul commented on this in 1 Corinthians 9:19: "Though I am free and belong to no man, I make myself a slave to everyone." "Second," Sue continued, "a man must be willing to have some of his own needs met by others."

We must stop trying to do everything by ourselves, while at the same time we must be sensitive to the needs of others. The result will be a happier, more meaningful life.

Happiness, if sought directly, however, will prove to be elusive. Don't seek friendships solely for selfish reasons. Look for and meet the needs of others; then and then alone will lasting friendships be established. Friendship, like so many good things in life, comes to those who are other-people centered.

Discussion Questions

1. Do you have one or two close Christian friends with whom you are committed by mutual agreement? If you must answer no, would you be willing to ask God to give to you at least one such friend?

2. When you first meet another man, by what criteria do you determine whether he could be a potential friend? Discuss what occurs in the crucial first four minutes of a new relationship. What makes these four minutes so important?

3. Do you agree that extraordinary friendships can be developed with very ordinary people? What are some benefits?

4. What do you imagine Will Rogers meant when he said, "I never met a man I didn't like"?

5. Discuss different ideas for developing new friendships that were not mentioned in this chapter.

Notes

Chapter 1
1. James Wagenvoord, ed., *Men: A Book for Women* (New York: Avon Books, 1978), p. 165.
Chapter 2
2. Dan Benson, *The Total Man* (Wheaton: Tyndale House Publishers, 1977), p. 15.
3. Benson, *The Total Man*, p. 15.
4. Wagenvoord, *Men: A Book for Women*, p. 166.
5. Sol Gordon, *Psychology for You* (New York: Oxford Book Company, 1972), p. 31.
Chapter 3
6. Margaret Mead, *Sex and Temperament in Three Primitive Societies* (New York: William Morrow and Company, Inc., 1963).
7. Boyce Rensberger, "What a Difference Sex Makes in Human Behavior," *Chicago Tribune*, December 24, 1978, p. 11. Copyrighted 1978, *Chicago Tribune*. Used with permission.
8. Ibid.
9. Sydney J. Harris, *The Best of Sydney J. Harris* (Boston: Houghton Mifflin Company, 1976), pp. 101,102.
Chapter 6
10. Herb Goldberg, *Hazards of Being Male: Surviving the Myth of Masculine Privilege* (New York: New American Library, 1977), p. 136.
11. Daniel Levinson, et. al., *The Seasons of a Man's Life* (New York:

Alfred A. Knopf, 1978), p. 335.

12. Joseph Bensman and Robert Zilienfeld, "Friendship and Aliena-
tion," *Psychology Today*, October 1979, p. 59.

13. Mary B. Parless, "The Friendship Bond," *Psychology Today*,
October 1979, p. 50. Copyright 1979 by Ziff-David Publishing Co.

14. Maxine Hancock, *The Forever Principle* (Old Tappan, NJ: Fleming H. Revell Co., 1980), p. 78.

Chapter 7

15. Robert Bell, *Worlds of Friendship* (Beverly Hills: Sage Publications, 1981), p.

16. George Santayana, in Robert R. Bell *Worlds of Friendship*
(Beverly Hills: Sage Publications, 1981), p. 96.

17. Merrill C. Tenney, ed., *Zondervan's Pictorial Bible Dictionary*
(Chicago: Zondervan Publishing House, 1969), p. 898.

18. Karen B. Mains, *Open Heart—Open Home* (Elgin, IL: David C.
Cook Publishing Comany, 1976), p. 21. Copyright 1976 by David C.
Cook Publishing Co. Used with permission.

Chapter 8

19. Mildred Newman and Bernard Berkowitz, *How to Be Your Own
Best Friend* (Boston: G.K. Hall and Sons, 1976), p.

20. O. Quentin Hyder, *The Christian's Handbook of Psychiatry* (Old
Tappan, NJ: Fleming H. Revell Co., 1971), p. 144. Used by permission.

21. A book that examines the problems and suppositions of psychology is Paul Vitz, *Psychology as Religion: The Cult of Self-Worship*
(Grand Rapids: William B. Eerdmans Publishing Comapny, 1977).

Chapter 9

22. Ralph W. Keyes, "We the Lonely People," *Intellectual Digest*,
December, 1973, p. 26.

23. Gary Collins, "Search of Christian Macho," *Moody Monthly*,
July-August, 1976), pp. 53-56. Adapted with permission from The
Secret of Our Sexuality, Gary Collins, ed. Copyright © 1976 by
Word, Inc.

24. Henry and Marion Jacobson, "The Sin Most Churches Deny,"
Moody Monthly, January 1981.

25. Larry Richards, "The Great American Congregation: The Illusive
Ideal?" *Christianity Today*, November 21, 1980, p. 23.

26. David Augsburger, *Caring Enough to Confront* (Ventura, CA:
Regal Books, 1980), p. 15.

Chapter 10

27. H. Norman Wright, *Seasons of a Marriage* (Ventura, CA: Regal

Books, 1982), p. 75.

28. Theodore I. Rubin, "What Women Don't Understand About Men," *Ladies' Home Journal*, September 1973, p. 24. © 1973 LHJ Publishing, Inc. Reprinted with permission of the author and *Ladies Home Journal*.

29. Dale Carnegie, *How to Win Friends and Influence People* (New York: Simon and Schuster, 1982). Original copyright 1936 by Dale Carnegie, renewed 1964 by Dorothy Carnegie.

30. S. Holly Stocking, Diana Arezzo and Shelly Leavitt, *Helping Kids Make Friends* (Allen, TX: Argus Communications, 1981).

31. Norman Vincent Peale, reprinted in *Indianapolis Star*, 1981 via Ann Ackers' featured syndicate.

32. Saul K. Padover, *Jefferson: A Great American Life and Ideas* (New York: Mentor Books, 1970), pp. 163,164.

33. Dale Carnegie, *How to Win Friends*, p. 146.

34. Harold H. Dawley, *Friendship: How to Make and Keep Friends* (Englewood Cliff, NJ: Prentice-Hall Inc., 1980), pp. 118,119.

Other Regal Books to help you build better relationships: